The Gift Giving Handbook
For The Inept Man

Thousands of Gift Giving Ideas To Make His Life Easier And Her Life Better

Timothy B. Schnabel

Shanem Publishing   **West Hollywood, California**

The Gift Giving Handbook For The Inept Man

Thousands of Gift Giving Ideas To Make His Life Easier And Her Life Better

By

Timothy B. Schnabel

Published By:

Shanem Publishing
8491 Sunset Blvd., #1700
West Hollywood, CA   90069   U.S.A.

ISBN: 0 – 9743765 – 8 – 2   LCCC#: 2003095363

To Olivia, Summer, and Shane; the greatest gifts God ever put in my life.

TABLE OF CONTENTS

Acknowledgement

The contributions made to this handbook were numerous and invaluable. I am truly grateful for all your wonderful stories, experiences, and insights. Without your help, this book could not have been completed. Much love and thanks to Paul & Deborah Savage, Danny Stephens, Courtney G. Belford, Daryl & Tanya Muncey, Wynne Cooper, Helaine Lembeck, Elizabeth O'Brien, Debbie Wilson, Mitchell Bank, Kathleen Sahar, Jon & Colleen Hazelbaker, Camille Farnsworth, Sally Stringer, Candice Jenkins, Jill Idzkowski, Jeff Schnabel, Paula Carder, Mary Kay Schnabel, Lee Schnabel, and John F. Schnabel.

Warning & Disclaimer

This book is designed to provide information in regard to the topic and subject matter covered. It is sold with the understanding the author and publisher are not engaged in rendering professional advice or services. At no point are this author and publisher attempting to give professional advice on relationships and personal interaction. Should expert assistance regarding the subject matter contained in these pages be needed, you are urged to seek a competent professional.

It is not the purpose of this handbook to reprint all information available on this subject or the entirety of relevant information available to this author and/or publisher. You are encouraged to read all information available in other sources to learn as much as possible about the subject matter.

The purpose of this handbook is to entertain. Every effort has been made to make this handbook as accurate and complete as possible. There may be typographical errors and/or mistakes in content. Shanem Publishing and the author shall not be liable nor responsible to any person or entity with respect to any loss or damage caused, or alleged to be caused, directly or indirectly by the information contained in this book.

If you do not wish to be bound by the above, please return this book to Shanem Publishing for a full refund.

Introduction

It is six o'clock in the evening and my third hour of mall shopping ends unproductively. Throngs of people drift by. I take a moment to dwell on everything I have seen and realize the holiday season has turned a myriad of individual personalities into a gaggle of goal oriented automatons. People seem to have fallen into two distinct categories: They are either blissfully and annoyingly happy or bitter angry jerks. At this point, I seem to have fallen into the latter category. It is not my fault, however, since all five hundred thousand people in this mall seem to be fighting for the three decent gifts left in the building. So far, the only bright spots of the experience were the traditional stop at the gourmet cookie store and the occasional well-placed massage chairs where I was able to sit for five minutes until the next battle weary man needed a break. Now, my back aches, my feet hurt, I feel lightheaded and my eyes are blurred over. I don't have the strength to fight off one more salesperson whose sole purpose in life is to attack me with perfume as I enter her store.

I decide to leave with one pathetic stocking stuffer to show for my day. In my car, I sit dumbfounded trying in vain to listen to some music. Thoroughly fried, my brain meanders desperately trying to figure out what gifts to buy, for whom, and how much to spend. My favorite CD is nothing but white noise over my thoughts. I cannot focus on anything other than the cramping in my legs. It is exasperating. I truly believe this goes against everything I am as a person. I do not want to talk to anyone or even see another person for the rest of the day. All I want to do is go home, kick off my shoes, take a hot shower to wash off the day, and pop open a beer or maybe three. Does any of this sound familiar?

Gift giving has been a part of the human experience for ages. As much as some people would hope, it shows no sign of stopping either. Gifts are given for romance, for sympathy, for guilt, for religion, for love, for special occasions, and sometimes even to get something in return. Gift giving is an important part of life. But that is not why I wrote this book.

Gift giving is an important way to show the significant people in your life how much they mean to you, whether they be your sweetheart, your wife, your parent, grandparent, siblings, other family members, or friends. While the emphasis in this book will be on gift giving for your sweetheart or spouse, the same principals apply to all the others.

But let us start with the wife or sweetheart, where a small token of affection given at just the right moment can go a long way toward letting her see how much you care about her and want her in your life. It shows how much you listen to her needs and billboards your desire to make her life more rewarding. But that too is not why I wrote this book.

Throughout my youth and adult life I dreamed about owning some sort of manual describing how to give just the right gift. I wanted an informational booklet filled with great gifts of all kinds to dazzle the vital person in my life. I wanted a place where I could find impressive gift ideas that she would fawn over. I wanted to have some idea about her wants, needs, likes, and dislikes well before I ever thought about going into a store. To be honest, I wanted my shopping experience to be no more painful than stopping to buy a pack of gum at the drugstore on my way home. That is why I wrote this book.

This is the book I dreamed about. You see... I am the Inept Man. Or, at least I was. I was a horrible gift giver. I looked at gift giving as another in a long line of obligations. It was a nuisance of immense proportion. I never knew what gift to buy and shopping was nothing more than an expensive guessing game. It was impossible for me to find anything matching the personality of the recipient and I found the stores lacking in the sheer variety of items available. Now in all fairness, it is hard to find great Christmas gifts when you wait until five o'clock on December twenty-fourth to go shopping. Be that as it may, I usually purchased the quickest thing I thought might be appropriate and half-heartedly wrapped it up just in time to hand it off to the beneficiary of this loving gesture. You can imagine how special she felt.

Gift giving was just one more annoyance taking a bite out of my time. I asked myself repeatedly why I was required to give gifts since I did not care to receive them all that much. I even felt guilty when I received a gift and felt I must return the gesture in order to purge that guilt. The whole process seemed dirty to me.

As I matured, I started realizing other people did not share my views. Gift giving is important to many people. Gary Chapman, author of *The Five Love Languages*, describes how many people utilize gift giving as their primary way to show affection. These people not only show their love by giving gifts but they feel deeply loved when receiving them.

Furthermore, I discovered how many people showing affection in other ways liked to enhance the experience by giving gifts. These people did not want anything in return. They just wanted to share their love and appreciation with the important people in their lives.

I grappled with this concept for quite a while. In fact, I refused gifts given to me simply because I did not have anything to give in return. To me, "Guilt" demanded a gift be given in exchange for any gift received. My mother broke me of this negative process by insisting, "If you do not receive a gift well, you take away the joy from a person who truly wants to show you how much you mean to them." This slowly sank in and allowed me to relax and absorb the love and affection without the panic of not having something to give back.

So, after I finally surrendered my giftaphobia, I decided to work on my gift giving skills. It took years. My gift giving ineptness was so ingrained that hundreds of mistakes inevitably happened before realizing my next series of problems. I was a procrastinator, neurotic, and unconfident. And I quickly found out I was not alone. In talking with other men, I found there is an overabundance out there with the same problems. In fact, my friends and I laughed at the mistakes we made. We commiserated about having to give gifts in the first place and how shopping was not our idea of a good time. We compared neurosis and lazy habits and laughed at the reaction each received when our significant others got horribly non-thought-out gifts. But one day, a woman nearby was listening and interjected. She said:

You know guys; there is more to gift giving than that. About two years ago I gave birth to my son. Within six months I was exhausted and did not know if I could do it anymore. The baby was sick and between his crying, worrying about his fever, and trying to feed him, sleep was hard to come by. I was worn out and almost delirious. My husband read the play. One afternoon he handed me an envelope with instructions. I had an appointment at five o'clock at a local spa. He had arranged a massage, a manicure, and a pedicure for me. After that, the instructions told me to go to the local hotel. I did as instructed and there was a room in my name. When I opened the door, there was basket with earplugs, a sleep mask, a bottle of Merlot, one wine glass, some snacks, and an envelope with enough money for dinner in the restaurant and a drink at the bar. The note also included notice a late checkout had been arranged and I was not to return to the house until after noon the next day.

She went on to say how her husband's gift was his way of saying he loved her and was concerned about her needs. After that, my friends and I just felt stupid.

So, my next task was to figure out exactly why I was a bad gift giver. Was I insensitive or just selfish? Was I lazy or did my fears about giving just the right gift make it seem that way. Did I hate shopping or did I just despise the hoards of clamoring people fighting for merchandise? What were my true issues? The truth: I did not take the time to really know whom I was buying for.

Observation is the most important trait a gift giver can possess. All anyone needs to become a good gift giver is the desire to learn about the passions, wishes, needs, likes, and dislikes of another person. After that, gift giving becomes quite easy. I am not saying gift giving becomes joyful, I am just saying it becomes easy.

One thing to consider is most men shop differently than women. Most men, myself included, like to have an idea of what we want prior to shopping. Shopping is a task, not an event. We like to drive to one store where the merchandise is located, rush in and pick out exactly the item we were looking for and rush out again. It is an errand to be run, not a relaxing day out.

> **Most men find moving from store to store, without any idea whatsoever, to be an exercise in futility.**

Most women on the other hand, and I know I am in grave danger of generalizing, like to shop. I know hundreds of women who love to peruse the malls and look at all the new trends. They love to wander in and out of each store, seeking just the right item to fit their wardrobe or home décor. Discount stores provide racks and boxes of sale items for them to dig through in the hopes of finding the proverbial "diamond in the rough." It is seemingly a great experience for them to sift through endless rows of merchandise, all waiting to be purchased and taken home.

It is with these specific differences in mind that I have written this book. This book is for all those men like me who want some idea of what to get our girlfriends and wives before we actually go shopping. Inside its pages are in-depth lists of potential gift ideas available for perusing during a few moments of free time. Take the time to leaf through and check off the gifts appropriate for your lover. Also, throughout the book are questions to be answered like, "What is her ring size?" and, "What is her favorite flower?" The questions exist to take the guesswork out of gift giving. Going into a jewelry shop armed with the knowledge of her favorite stone, her birthstone, her ring size, her neck size, her wrist size, her favorite necklace length and so on will make shopping in that venue as pain free as possible. The same goes for clothing stores, flower shops, and all the other stores. I guarantee you, if you take the time to answer all the questions in this book, gift giving will become far easier than you ever imagined.

And ladies, help your man answer the questions. This does not have to feel like a homework assignment to him. The goal is for him to enjoy shopping for you, or at the very least shop for you with far less dread. You will ultimately be on the receiving end of his newly found knowledge and experience. The more data he has about you, the more appropriate and imaginative gifts you will receive. Also, envision how your life might improve if he truly starts enjoying the process. Although the likelihood of men ever learning to love the shopping experience is remote, with the help of this book and a little effort, gift giving should become much easier for him and more fulfilling for both of you.

Gift Giving Rules

Rule #1
Stick to the Romantic Gifts

Rule #2
Go back and reread Rule #1

Rule #3
Listen to her. She is not secretive. She wants good gifts and will let you know what they are.

Rule #4
Open your eyes. Everything you need to know is right in front of you.

Rule #5
Failure is inevitable. Don't worry about it. Just accept it and move on.

Chapter 1

An Apology to Women

Men, the first real question should be "Is an apology really necessary?" Well, you will have to decide that for yourself. Now I realize shopping goes against our nature. I know we would rather come home and tell our significant others we like them a whole bunch and they should be content with that. I know many of us work very hard to bring home the bacon, mow the yard, take out the trash, and all we ask in return is a little loving and an occasional word of praise. Well my fellow Neanderthals, it is time to come out of the cave.

Even while writing this book, many men asked the simple question, "Why should we have to be the ones to give gifts?" My answer was simply, "You don't. Just get used to being single." Now I realize this oversimplifies relationships. It makes all relationships seem like they survive or fail by the type and frequency of the gifts the females receive. This is just not true. It is true, however, that women like to feel appreciated. Gift giving can be a rewarding way for us to express our love for the women in our lives. It lets them know they mean as much to us as we mean to them. It is a necessary part of the relationship to let them know we think about them on a daily basis. Giving a gift can sometimes be the perfect way to express emotions words cannot do adequately. It helps them feel loved. It is therefore horribly thoughtless and irresponsible to not give gifts. And yet, most of us fail miserably at it. So, is an apology necessary? Why not?

To all those women who care so much about their man that they find ways to make him feel loved, and who only want to feel appreciated every so often themselves, we apologize for our lack of understanding. For our thoughtless oversight of your devotion, we pledge to do better in our quest to become a more caring person. We will try to break the molds of our upbringing and learn to find out what is important in your life and strive to present you with more meaningful gestures of our love and admiration. In other words... don't expect too much, but we'll give it a shot.

Chapter 2

Why Most Men Stink At Gift Giving

First, let me pay tribute to the few men out there who mastered the art of gift giving and continually please the women they care about. Yes ladies, they do exist. Unlike Bigfoot and the Loch Ness Monster, men who give great gifts do live and breathe. They are, however, as elusive as the aforementioned creatures. But when you find one, you will be rewarded with precious sentiment and thoughtfulness like you have never been accustomed.

Gifts are visual symbols of love, whether they are items you purchased or made, or are merely your own presence made available to your spouse. Gifts demonstrate that you care, and they represent the value of the relationship.

- Gary Chapman, Author
The Five Love Languages

Men who know how to give gifts truly enjoy pleasing their significant other. These men give presents for the sole purpose of letting their lovers, their wives, and their friends know how much their existence is valued. These men instinctively know what pleases their partner and they take time to make each present meaningful.

> **Most superior gifts are personalized and have something to do with the way you feel about her.**

Sadly, in researching this book I have encountered frightening stories of inappropriate gifts, untimely gifts, and simple complaints about no gifts at all. I too have an extensive and forgettable history of giving unfortunate gifts. I witnessed first hand the reactions, or should I say "fallout," from normally delightful women to gifts carelessly thought-out and horribly presented.

So why do we fail so badly? Why are we so horribly inept? It's not like the women we live with avoid giving us clues. It's not like they remain horribly secretive about their likes and dislikes. It's not like a nondescript gift would fail to improve their day. So what is our problem?

There are unfortunately many answers to this question. The first is "procrastination." This is probably the most common of all gift-giving flaws. Some men are so busy in their own worlds trying to get ahead in their chosen careers they do

What are her ring sizes?

Ring Finger: _____

Pinky Finger: _____

Third Finger: _____

Second Finger: _____

Thumb: _____

not seem to find time to go shopping. After working forty hours a week or more, the last thing they want to do is fight some disgusting crowd in a mall to find a gift they cannot afford in the first place. The task is shelved until the last possible moment before rushing out to buy the first thing they think might be appropriate. Unfortunately, most gifts purchased in this hasty manner feel exactly that way to the women receiving them. These busy men don't realize how limiting their caring to the last few minutes of the day has little chance of impressing their partner.

"Laziness" is procrastination taken to the nth level. The main difference is that procrastination does not rule out the possibility of true caring. Laziness indicates the man's free time, or rest time, is more important than shopping for his lover. Ironically, many of the gifts given by the lazy man are far superior to those given by the procrastinator. The procrastinator's gift usually reflects some half-hearted attempt to purchase something his partner might actually need or identify with. The lazy man's gift, if he gets one at all, is usually something quick and big. There is no real thought and hardly any shopping involved, just a credit card and one quick trip to the store. Look at it this way, although most of the lazy man's gifts have no sentimental value, sometimes a new television set, a new VCR, a new car, or some expensive jewelry can be just what the doctor ordered.

The gift I want more than any other is for him to go to therapy.
- Jill Idzkowski

"Neurosis" is the most interesting reason men fail to give wonderful gifts. In fact, shopping becomes a nightmarish venture for some men. This used to be my fatal flaw as well. I very much wanted to give my partner just the right gift but became terribly apprehensive she already had one, she would not be able to use it, she would not like it, or one of many other possible scenarios. I got bogged down in the process. I was so upset about not knowing what to get I became virtually incapable of getting anything.

For the neurotic man, good gift ideas are like gold. The neurosis has no chance of kicking in if he does not have to think for himself. And if you are one of the neurotics out there, remember this one thing: If she does not like the gift, she will still like you for thinking about her. It is better than not giving a gift at all.

Note to Men

If you do not know what to get her, or you are unsure if she would like a particular gift, call her girlfriends. They will most definitely know her likes and dislikes, and they might even come up with some new gift ideas for you.

Finally, the reason some men are so dreadful is not a function of caring, it is not a function of overwork, and it is not even a function of time. Some men are just cheap. They think a relationship should stand on its own merit and they should not have to buy gifts all the time to prove their love. There is little I can say to help these men. They just do not understand the value some people place on receiving gifts and probably never will.

Note to Women

Observe your man to find out his gift-giving flaws. If he is neurotic, take him shopping with you and point out the things you like. If he procrastinates, give him a list of gift ideas in advance and locations to find the items. If he is lazy and cheap and you want better gifts, just get a new man.

Buying a gift for a woman can be a tremendous boost for the relationship or a tremendous bust. The right gift reminds her you are paying attention. It lets her know you have her needs in mind and you care a great deal about her. If you have one of the above flaws, it is never too late to change the behavior. Take small steps and watch her reaction. Her positive feedback might be all you need to permanently change into an enlightened and skilled giver.

Chapter 3

It Is The Thought That Counts: Yeah, Right!

In fact, it is the size, shape, expense, style, color and timeliness, etc. that counts and you had better not forget it. Many advertisers even use the slogan *It is the thought that counts* when selling their products. They insist the best way to show your caring is to buy their product rather than their competitors. Although this is not the same meaning your mother might place on the slogan, it is probably a more accurate depiction of current culture.

> **Money makes it easier to buy gifts, but does not necessarily make them better gifts**

We are judged in so many different ways by the types of gifts we buy. This hardly seems fair since we are doing a very nice thing. We should be allowed to give her a gift without any baggage or judgments associated with it. We should be able to simply present her the gift, get the requisite amount of adulation and move on with our daily lives. I have bad news for you fellas. It doesn't work that way.

Start Small. If you start with big gifts like jewelry and cars, they quickly learn to expect it and you have nowhere to go from there but down.

- **Jon Hazelbaker**

Judgments come in all shapes and sizes, just like the gifts they refer to. What does the gift mean? Does the gift seem like a last minute or obligatory gift? Is the gift appropriate? Does the gift show you were thinking about her or is it just a random gift with no emotional significance? Is the gift supposed to be an apology? Is there a hidden agenda behind giving the gift? Is the gift cheap or does the price adequately reflect the importance of the relationship? Was the gift given at the right time? Will this gift impress her friends? Does this gift mean she has to reciprocate? And there are many, many more.

> **Observation is the most important trait a gift giver can possess.**

If there is one thing becoming crystal clear throughout the investigation of this book, it is the undeniable fact that women need to feel appreciated by their men. It is imperative for us to let them know we think of them often, understand their needs, and value their presence in our lives. Therefore, any gift we give either adds to or subtracts from the value of the relationship. A well thought-out gift shows we understand her desires and lets her know how deeply we care. Conversely, a last minute inappropriate gift can make her feel less loved and appreciated.

The greatest gifts carry with them lots of sentiment. Gifts that profess your love mean more than any other.

- **Kathleen Sahar**

Perhaps these random judgments happen because human beings are so instinctually insecure. While the great well thought-out gifts boost and validate self-worth, poorly thought-out gifts or insignificant gestures serve to negatively impact self-esteem. To avoid these random judgments, a gift with meaning should naturally take into account the flavor of the individual it is purchased for. It should reflect her passions, desires, needs, and wants. A gift of much less thought might reflect someone else's tastes.

What is her favorite color?

_____

Regardless of the reasons judgments exist, don't let them detour you from becoming a great gift giver. Just remember to do what you think is right. Ultimately, you have no control over what the other person thinks. If you are buying a gift because you truly want to make her feel special, odds are she will take it that way. If you are trying to get something from her by buying a gift, odds are she will know that too. Most people can sense the intent of the giver. They know if a gift was purchased out of convenience, obligation, friendship, love, or passion. Do not expect a gift given out of convenience to get the same response as one given out of love.

The good news is that judgments cut both ways. Great gift givers are not only judged favorably by their significant others, but by her friends as well.

What are her favorite perfumes?

_____

_____

_____

Make no mistake; giving great gifts is a skill. Once you become an expert craftsman, you might find yourself the benchmark by which her friends judge their own husbands.

Chapter 4

Card Giving: The First Battlefield

Card giving may seem like a relatively easy thing to do. There are thousands of card shops, gift shops, novelty shops, drug stores, grocery stores, and even convenience stores with racks of cards just waiting for you. Finding a location to purchase a card is clearly not an issue. Finding just the right card inside those venues is most likely quite simple too. So what possible difficulties could there be?

I guess the first issue is knowing when to buy a card. The answer: Every chance you get!   The obvious occasions for card buying are birthdays and holidays. These occasions are very important and a heart-felt card does wonders to make your significant other feel important. But occasions like these are not the only time you should buy a card. You see, birthdays and most holidays carry with them the obligation of card and gift giving. Even though card giving at these times is nice and appreciated, the cards are nevertheless expected. If this book teaches you anything, it is that cards and gifts coming out of left field often mean so much more than the obligatory ones.

Say your spouse gets up in the morning and stubs her toe on the bedside dresser. Her toenail turns black and blue and hurts a great deal. Maybe she even broke it. How do you think she will feel when you come home from work with a card

What size necklace does she prefer?

☐ Choker ☐ Medium
☐ Short ☐ Long

What is her neck size?

saying, "Sorry you got hurt," and carrying a bouquet of her favorite flowers? It may not fix her toe, but rest assured she will be very pleased you were thinking about her all day.

What about a girlfriend who just dropped a lifelong friendship because of a huge argument? She will no doubt be questioning herself and the choices she made. How do you think she would feel getting a card saying, "You are a wonderful person and I just wanted you to know how special you are?" This could go a long way toward easing her pain. And not to mention, you will look better in the process.

Simply put, find reasons to give cards. If nothing major happens in her life, make something up. If she seems bored, give her a card to break the boredom. If she appears tired, give her a card to perk her up. Even if you find her happy and content, a card will undoubtedly add to her mood. Take the time to send the message you love her and think about her. She will respond favorably.

Note to Men

Do not forget Electronic E-cards as a viable card giving option to
brighten her day. But be aware, a purchased card inside
an envelope carries much more sentimental value.

The second issue is about those men not comfortable with writing their own words and feelings? Never fear, there are thousands of cards out there. All the major card makers and manufacturers have hundreds of employees coming up with almost anything you could possibly want or need to say. It just takes a little extra time to search the card racks to find a card adequately reflecting the emotions you want to convey to your loved one. If you cannot find what you are looking for at one store, go to another. You will find what you are looking for if you just take the time to do it.

Another option might be giving your own words a try anyway. Many cards are created with a blank page for your unique and personal thoughts. Even if you find yourself uncomfortable with your emotions, are not sure exactly how to put them into words or just hate your own handwriting, a personal message can be very intimate and rewarding. Simply imagine the words, "I Love You." Is it more satisfying for you to read those three words from a typed piece of paper or handwritten from someone you care deeply about?

The final issue in picking out the right card came to my attention in the not too distant past. One woman, when receiving a birthday card said, "That is very nice, but it really is a man's card." I had no idea what she was talking about. She explained that the autumn color scheme on the front of the card represented the giver (me) and not the receiver (her). She explained the earth tones

What jewelry does she most like to wear?	
☐ Rings	☐ Bracelets
☐ Necklaces	☐ Piercings
☐ Earrings	☐ Pendants
☐ Watches	☐ Brooches

on the front of the card made it represent a man instead of having nice pastels, pinks, flowers, etc. which represent a woman. Since I was purchasing the card for a woman, I needed the card to reflect a woman.

First, let me go on record to say that I still believe her to be insane. My feeling was simply, "You got a card. Be grateful and shut up about it." However, my neurosis kicked in and I started wondering whether there was something to her statement. Is a card supposed to represent the giver or the receiver? Now I know a gift is supposed to be something the receiver wants. It is not proper etiquette to send a gift you desire and then use it when she sets it aside. However, is it the card's cover or the inside message which is supposed to reflect the person receiving the card, or both?

I started worrying about this question and had no real answers of my own. I did, however, find it very difficult to pick out cards from that point on. When I went card shopping, I looked at pictures of serene nature scenes, little boys, and puppies followed by pictures of flowers, little girls with umbrellas, and kittens. I wondered for whom I would purchase each card. Did the flowers represent the woman receiving the card or did it say the card was from a woman? If I sent a card with a beautiful tree lined hiking trail, did it say the card is for a man or from one? What if she likes dogs? Am I to still send her a card with flowers on it? What about the pictures of scenic overlooks, nature cards, colorful non-specific art type cards, floral arrangements, ocean scenes, little fuzzy animals, etc.? I was finding it very difficult to enjoy the card giving process because I could not really get an answer to the question, "What is appropriate?"

I decided to do some research. I went on a fact-finding mission and asked many of the people I know. I polled both women and men on this journey. I asked them which types of cards they preferred and if it mattered what was really on the cover. The answer I received turned out to be quite pleasing for me. Most of them had never even thought about this before. They all received cards in the past and were very appreciative. They never really considered what was on the front. Unanimously they agreed, "She got a card. She should be grateful and shut up about it!"

Cards are designed to send a message of love and caring. If someone judges you on the type of card you send, that might say more about her than it does about you. Pick out a card that represents what you feel inside. If it genuinely reflects your feelings, the person receiving it should be quite happy with the gesture. If you think she will like one card over another, send it to her. Don't worry about it. Just taking the time to send your love is all that really matters.

Note to Men

Buy numerous cards for different occasions in advance. This way, you do not have to rush out to card shop every time something new arises.

<u>**Horror Story #116**</u>

The Dog Bone

Debbie, a very dear friend of mine, had been talking about getting a puppy for several months. She had not acted on it, but was truly interested in one day acquiring a cute little ball of fluff for companionship. As her birthday approached, her boyfriend of over three years decided to give her a present along that theme. When her birthday arrived, he showed up at her apartment carrying a nicely wrapped gift in his hands. It was obviously not the puppy she had been asking for; rather it was a small wrapped box that rattled when she shook it. They sat down together and she slowly tore open the packaging. Inside, and much to her surprise, was a doggy chew toy. She looked at him, mildly confused, and asked why she was given this particular gift. Proudly, he explained how he knew she wanted a puppy and when she gets it, the dog will have a toy to chew on.

Unfortunately, that $1.99 squeaky rubber item represented the entirety of her gifts for that birthday from her boyfriend. She did not get a romantic gift and she did not even get the puppy. But at least she has some cheap new clutter to adorn her apartment.

Chapter 5

Men Are Not Blind Or Stupid, We Just Act Like We Are

How many men buy gifts for their wives and girlfriends and hear phrases like, "Why did you think I would like this?" or "Who were you thinking of when you bought this?" or my favorite, "This is great. Did you keep the receipt?"

Fellas, we all know failure is expected and predictable. It is not possible to delight her with every idea we come up with. In fact, half the time she changes her mind about things she thinks she wants in the first place. Be that as it may, the fact that failure is occasionally expected does not mean we are permitted to fall short every time. We must learn why we fail so often and attempt to fix the problem.

> Any gift can backfire. We all know a mood could strike or a gift could hit her the wrong way for no reason at all. Just be prepared for that inevitability and move on.

It is important to realize that all women have their own unique style. They have their individual likes, dislikes, tastes, preferences, and needs that separate them from other women. A man need only pay attention to determine what clothing she likes, what perfume she wears, what music she listens to and what possessions she already owns.

There is a concept I call, "The Clayton Factor." My friends Paul and Debbie Savage have been married for seven years and have an adorable two-year-old son named Clayton. Extremely cute and full of energy, Clayton is now learning his first few words. Sitting in their living room the other day I noticed Clayton walking in from the kitchen holding an empty wine glass. Proudly, he held it up in the air and announced the word, "Mommy." Everyone in the room busted out laughing. You see one of Debbie's great passions is good wine. She often has a glass with her meals and enjoys a glass or two while relaxing by the fireplace in the evening. Clayton knew nothing of her knowledge and passion for wine; he just knew a wine glass reminded him of his mom.

Paul went on to describe Clayton's behavior in a clothing store earlier that week. As is typical for Paul, he wanted to surprise Debbie with something to wear so he grabbed his son and headed for the department stores. As they shopped, each time Clayton saw an article of clothing with a leopard pattern, he pointed and again announced, "Mommy." As you suspect, Debbie loves the leopard pattern on furniture, clothing, and miscellaneous accessories.

Now fellas, if a two year old who can barely walk and say only a few words is capable of looking at an item and knowing his mom would like it, how embarrassing is it for us to say we have no clue about the woman in our lives? All we really need to do is open our eyes.

Note to Women

Do not wait for your man's observation skills to kick in by themselves. If you know what you want and he does not pick up on subtle clues, get more direct.

Try an experiment. Close your eyes right now and picture your significant other's apartment, house, etc. What colors permeate the rooms? What style is her furniture? When you opened the refrigerator to get a beer, what kind of food did she have in it? What did her bathroom look like? Does she have candles? What scent? What color? Does she wear perfume? If you can picture these things in your head, you are half the way toward becoming a very successful gift giver.

Think back to the last time you went for a walk with your sweetheart. As you walked, did she mention any of her likes or dislikes? Did you happen to walk by a store window and look in? Did she see anything she thought was pretty? Have you ever taken a drive and seen a new restaurant she said she would love to try? Has she ever casually mentioned a city she would like to visit or a sport she always wanted to experience? The clues come at random times and can be about virtually anything.

On a walk with a former girlfriend on a brisk autumn evening, we smelled the smoke from a fireplace nearby. She grabbed my arm, nestled up next to me and said, "I love this time of year. The smell of a fireplace makes me think of home." It did not take but seconds to realize anytime I wanted to put her in a nostalgic mood I needed only to build a fire for her. She could sit in front of it wrapped in a warm blanket and take a nice trip down memory lane. I could add to the moment by lighting vanilla scented candles, playing her favorite new age music, and popping a bowl of popcorn for her.

For those men concerned their significant other does not give those kinds of clues, keep your ears open. As mentioned previously, it is not like women are horribly secretive. They are not stupid when it comes to hinting. If they want gifts and are smart about it, they go out of their way to let you know exactly what they want. Odds are from this point forward you will hear more than you ever hoped to.

Note to Men

If she mentions she likes a dress in a store window, file the information away. Go back at your next opportunity, when she is not with you, to pick it up. Surprise her with it someday in the future.

Women also drop hints about what they do not want. Many times they hide suggestions in the context of other people. Things like: "Can you believe Betty got a dishwasher for her birthday? Who would want that?" or, "I don't understand why Jerry didn't give Elizabeth jewelry for their tenth wedding anniversary. He seems a little thoughtless." These are not idle conversations. They are direct clues for you to pick up on and she knows it.

If a woman mentions a gift one of her friends did or did not receive, she is undoubtedly making reference to her own likes and dislikes.

Even if you have a quiet unassuming girlfriend who does not speak about her desires all too often, look around. All needed information about your significant other is readily available to you. The clothing she wears, the furnishings she surrounds herself with, and the things she does for recreation all scream her individual preferences. Get to know who you are dealing with and painful statements like, "Gosh, I bet your ex-girlfriend would have loved this," will be kept to a minimum.

Chapter 6

Obligatory Gift Giving Days

Thankfully for us inept men, there are hundreds of days each year unrestrained by gift giving responsibilities. We are free to go about our lives without the excruciating pain and frustrations associated with gift shopping. The following days, however, do not carry such a carefree state of existence. Why? Because if you have someone important in your life, and want to keep them in your life, you are obliged to give them gifts on these specific days each and every year. You have no choice and there is little you can do about it. So you might as well quit complaining, suck it up, and go shopping.

What are her two favorite holidays?

_____   _____

February 14th – Valentine's Day

Women have no sense of humor when it comes to Valentine's Day. If you have a wife, a girlfriend, a lover, or you are casually dating someone, you have no alternative but to recognize this day by giving her something special and heartfelt. If you forget or just choose not to bestow on her a loving memento of your affections, God help you.

Flowers and candy are the traditional gifts for this day but there are many other romantic items out there for you to consider. Although many women said they enjoyed getting flowers each year, others thought it showed a lack of creativity. They enjoyed the gift but there was no special feeling associated with it anymore. They knew they were going to get a bouquet of long stem red roses every year and there was little or no inspiration on their husband's part.

Any gift can get boring if it is given year after year

Not to imply that women do not love getting flowers and candy, but any man can run to the flower shop and pick up some flowers on his way home from work. You can be more creative than that. It is just a matter of asking the question, "What makes your sweetheart feel loved?" When you think of your wife, what does she consider romantic? What would make her feel all warm and fuzzy? What would let her know you still have deep feelings of love for her?

Above all other holidays, a Valentine's Day gift should be of a romantic, sexy, and intimate nature.
                                        - Courtney G. Belford

Giving her a gift basket filled with massage lotions, bath beads and gels, a bottle of her favorite wine, some European gourmet chocolates, and a note telling her what she means to you might be one new idea. How about a romantic candlelit picnic in the snow (not a very good idea if she hates the cold.) Try giving her a spa day. And when she returns home feeling wonderful about herself, she can see how you cleaned the house and placed a romantic dinner for two on the table. There are so many ways to make her happy. Just be a little original and it will likely pay off bigtime.

A friend of mine dated a woman who doodled on napkins to pass the time whenever they went drinking. Before leaving each bar, he secretly collected the drawings. One Valentine's Day, she opened a gift wrapped box and was shocked to see a large picture frame with a year's worth of her doodles arranged in a collage. She was overwhelmed. When I asked her what was so wonderful about the gift, she replied, "He was thinking about me every time we went out for the whole year. It just shows how much he loves me."

I am not suggesting you mesmerize her every year, but you can certainly find out what is important to her. If her idea of romance is a quiet evening together, clear your schedule and rent a movie together. The gift of your time can be more important to her than anything else you can think of. If food turns her on, take her for a nice romantic dinner to her favorite out-of-the-way restaurant. If physical touch is important to her, give her a massage and tell her how much she means to you. Many times, the simple gifts go the farthest.

Birthdays

Some women love to celebrate their birthdays with reckless abandon while others are more sensitive to growing older. Many women like being surrounded by family and friends while others like their birthdays to go by relatively unnoticed. No matter what she prefers with regard to how other people in her life celebrate it, you are not permitted to let her birthday slip by.

Birthday gifts cover a wide range. They can be something she needs or something she wants. Gifts for this day do not necessarily have to be romantic. Birthdays and Christmas allow you to be spontaneous, creative,

> **On her birthday, does she like to:**
>
> ☐ Celebrate Publicly
> ☐ Surround herself with only family and friends
> ☐ Celebrate quietly with you
> ☐ Avoid celebrating

clever, surprising, and humorous with regard to the gifts you give. Or, you can even surrender creativity and give her something she deliberately asked you for.

David, another long time friend of mine, dated a woman who wore the wackiest and loudest hats I have ever seen. She loved them and, because of her free spirit, was able to pull off the look quite well. One evening, David smuggled her favorite hat from the apartment and embarked on a mini-crusade. Over an entire weekend, he dragged the hat to every one of her friends and took pictures of them wearing it. He also went to her parents' house and took pictures of them modeling it as well. The next time he went to her apartment, he smuggled the hat back into her closet unnoticed. A month later, for her birthday, she unwrapped a picture frame with all the crazy hat people. To this day she loves the picture and more importantly tells the story over and over again to anyone seeing it.

If you are looking for a day to give her an original gift, this is it. Birthdays can be fun and wacky. Anything goes. With a little bit of effort, you can find a unique way to celebrate her special day. And trust me, anything you do that is fun and a little out of character will be a nice surprise and greatly appreciated.

DISCLAIMER

While interviewing, many women said they would rather have romantic gifts for every holiday. It is important for them to feel love from their partners on their birthday as well as on Valentine's Day and Anniversaries. As the gift giver, you must decide for yourself whether your sweetheart would like something original, wacky, useful, or heartfelt. If you do not know what she would like, you can ask her. But if asking will ruin the surprise element, include a little romantic something on top of the plans she knows about. But most of all don't sweat it. Odds are she will enjoy the fact you recognized her special day in the first place.

Wedding Anniversary

This day is the epitome of romance. It is not the day to be shunned, ignored, or forgotten. This day commemorates one of the biggest events in a couple's lives. A wedding is the culmination of two people's love and desire for each other and the first step toward fulfilling a promise to spend the rest of their lives together. How could anyone even think about not celebrating a day like this?

> **Forgetting a wedding anniversary is the largest gift giving blunder a man could ever commit**

Lucky for us men, wedding anniversaries are unique and have pre-determined guidelines for the gifts to be given. If you look at the next page, you will see a list of the traditional gifts versus the contemporary gifts for each of the major wedding anniversaries. Now remember, these are just general themes. It is up to you to craft them into creative gift ideas.

Wedding Anniversary Gifts

Traditional Gifts

First – Paper
Second – Cotton
Third – Leather
Fourth – Fruit / Flowers
Fifth – Wood
Sixth – Candy / Iron
Seventh – Wool / Copper
Eighth – Bronze / Pottery
Ninth – Pottery / Willow
Tenth – Tin / Aluminum
Eleventh – Steel
Twelfth – Silk / Linen
Thirteenth – Lace
Fourteenth – Ivory
Fifteenth – Crystal
Twentieth – China
Twenty-Fifth – Silver
Thirtieth – Pearl
Thirty-Fifth – Coral
Fortieth – Ruby
Forty-Fifth – Sapphire
Fiftieth – Gold
Fifty-Fifth – Emerald
Sixtieth – Diamond

Contemporary Gifts

First – Clocks / Plastics
Second – China / Calico
Third – Crystal / Glass
Fourth – Appliances / Books
Fifth – Silverware
Sixth – Candy / Iron
Seventh – Desk Sets
Eighth – Bronze / Pottery
Ninth – Linen / Lace
Tenth – Leather/Diamond Jewelry
Eleventh – Jewelry / Accessories
Twelfth – Pearls / Colored Gems
Thirteenth – Textiles / Furs
Fourteenth – Gold Jewelry
Fifteenth – Watches
Twentieth – Platinum
Twenty-Fifth – Silver
Thirtieth – Diamond
Thirty-Fifth – Jade
Fortieth – Ruby
Forty-Fifth – Sapphire
Fiftieth – Gold
Fifty-Fifth – Emerald
Sixtieth - Diamond

The traditional wedding gift for the first anniversary is paper. This does not mean you can wake up before her, walk to the front steps, and bring her the daily newspaper so she can read it first. You might try it, but good luck getting to the second anniversary. Why not spend some time finding a paper product reflecting her desires, moods, passions, or romantic aspirations? It may sound difficult, but it is not. There are a myriad of products out there she would love to have. Stationary, paper dolls, collectibles, antique books, hobby supplies, money, paper airline tickets, etc.

If you don't have any ideas on your own, visit the shopping malls, the local gift shops, and even scan the classified ads in your local newspaper. Why not log onto the Internet? Within seconds a search for the words, "wedding anniversary," rendered five hundred and fifty-two thousand websites. Most were designed with sales of appropriate wedding gifts in mind.

Your most important task, however, is discovering what makes her unique and therefore finding gifts she will truly enjoy receiving. And don't forget, on this day we receive gifts from her as well. The more extraordinary we make her feel every year, the more she will likely make us feel in return. It is a delightful win/win situation.

For those in loving relationships, this day is tremendously important. It can be equally important to those in unhappy marriages. It is all too apparent how life becomes difficult and challenging for those people caught in unhappy situations, but this day should not be overlooked even then. A well thought-out gift could be the first step toward mending some fences in bad need of repair.

Mother's Day

This is an important day to women with children. There is no greater bond in the world than between a mother and her offspring.   Ironically, a childless woman in West Virginia by the name of Anna Jarvis created this holiday in 1914. She tried to fight the commercialization of her creation but it was not surprisingly exploited by business.

This day is one of those semi-obligatory days since technically it is not you who are responsible for the gift giving. It is supposed to be recognized by the children. That being said, you are still duty-bound to orchestrate the plans, help purchase the gifts, and make sure the children are as well behaved as possible. And if you have infants, it is entirely up to you to recognize the tremendous effort and sacrifice of mothering your brood.

Gifts coming from the children can be anything, whereas gifts given by you should be as romantic as anniversary gifts. The most important thing is to let her know how significant she is to the family. Take some time to come up with a fun plan for her and the children, and then maybe plan a little something extra for after the kids go to bed.

Christmas & Chanukah

In our adult lives, Christmas joy and fascination might seem to be a distant memory. It appears the holidays are filled with blissfully and annoyingly happy people or frustrated angry jerks. Christmas seems more like a battle against parking, overcrowded stores, hostile customers, and picked through merchandise than it does about the birth of Christ and the love of family. This is even truer if you wait until December 24th to go shopping.

> Not every gift is going to be romantic. You will need to buy many "filler" gifts to give her multiple things to open and to enhance the entire gift giving experience.

Believe it or not, Christmas is really the easiest time of year to buy gifts. Every manufacturer fills the store shelves with new items and old favorites in the hopes you find just the right thing to buy. And just for your information, they do not wait until late December to put these items on the shelves. My mother owned a gift shop and would do her Christmas ordering in July so she could have the Christmas products on the shelf by mid October. Like her, most retail outlets want the products on the shelves early. They want anyone interested in buying great Christmas gifts to have ample time to find them. This is not a well-kept secret, even though in my inept days I had no knowledge of it.

BIG HINT

Shop for Christmas before Thanksgiving. Most gift items have already been stocked and virtually nobody will be shopping for them yet.

The day after Thanksgiving is the largest shopping day of the year. Christmas is the next big holiday on the calendar and the family is most likely together in one place. It is so much easier to shop for your family when they go along and point out what they like. You don't have the same luxury when it comes to buying for a significant other. Most women like surprises and do not want to point out every gift they are to receive. It is not as much fun opening presents if you already know what is inside. There are some exceptions:

> My friend Helaine was Christmas shopping and discovered a great pair of diamond earrings. Suspecting her husband would never find them again in such a big store, she purchased them on her own. She took them home, wrapped them beautifully, handed them to her husband and said, "Give these to me for Christmas." As an afterthought she commented, "By the way, you still have to pay for them when the bill arrives."

If you don't have a helpful wife who often does your shopping for you, you have no alternative but to venture out and shop alone. If you wait until the day after Thanksgiving, encountering the hordes of gift shoppers and "lookie-loos" is a guarantee. To avoid them, go shopping the week before Thanksgiving. Most items are on the shelves and ready to be looked through. There will likely be very few shoppers in relation to the following weeks and you will have first crack at anything you want.

Note to Men

You get presents on this holiday too. If you go shopping before her, you will see hundreds of things you want for yourself. This will make her life easier and your gifts better.

On the eight days of Chanukah, gifts are given predominately to the children. Usually a small gift or a little money is given on each of the eight nights. Although different families handle the celebration of this event in different ways, this is not a time to forget your significant other. Gifts for this holiday can be very romantic but they don't have to be. The style of gifts for Chanukah is just like style of gifts for Christmas in that respect. Just make sure you have something for her to open to reinforce how important she is in your life.

The key is not to wait until you have only a few choices. It may seem like work to go shopping for Christmas and Chanukah so early in the year but think how you feel the moment all your shopping is done. You can carry that feeling with you throughout the month of December and you too can be one of those blissful and annoyingly happy people.

One last comment about these obligatory days: They do not have to be filled with dread. I realize the word "obligation" has a negative connotation but it should not feel that way. For gosh sakes, we are in a relationship. Hopefully, we are in love and truly enjoy her and what she has to offer us intellectually, emotionally, and physically. If so, shopping for her should be joyous. Taking the time to plan a wonderful surprise or an original gift should be an undertaking bringing us great pride and satisfaction. We should enjoy how this woman, who means so much to us, will feel special because of our originality and thoughtfulness.

All that being said... I am a guy too. Sometimes obligation feels like obligation. For those times, suck it up and go shopping.

Miscellaneous Favorites

Only by getting to know your significant other in great detail will you be able to create an environment where new and exciting gift ideas jump out at you with ease.

What are her favorite fruits? _____ _____

_____ _____

What is her favorite chocolate? _____

What are her favorite snack foods? _____ _____

What is her favorite food? _____

What are her favorite restaurants? _____ _____

_____ _____

What are her favorite drinks? _____ _____

What is her favorite cookie? _____

What is her favorite cake? _____

What is her favorite pie? _____

Chapter 7

Non-Obligatory Gift Giving Days

Right about now you have to be asking yourself if this is really necessary. You just got done worrying about all the required holidays and now here come some more days to add to your list. Although buying a gift for every possible opportunity would mean doing little else with your time but shopping and wrapping, I do offer the suggestion that anyone can be a good gift giver on the holidays. It is the other days, the random inconsequential days, that can make the biggest impact.

It has been so long since I received a gift, I would be happy getting a toothpick with a bow on it right now.
- Mary Kay Schnabel

Non-obligatory gift-giving days are those days during the year with no real significance to the masses. The only importance associated with these days is of a personal nature between you and your significant other. No one else probably knows of, nor cares about, these particular days and would not notice if you let them slip by. For that matter, your wife or girlfriend might not even remember these days if you forgot about them. So why are they important? Non-obligatory gift-giving days are the days you show your honey she is special to you all year-round and not just on the days she is supposed to be important to you.

First Date Anniversary

How impressed will she be if you remember the time and place of your first date? Most women do not even remember this day and few couples celebrate it. I can tell you a small gift to remind her what that day meant to you might enhance how much she feels loved. Isn't this the goal of a happy healthy relationship?

First Kiss Anniversary

Again, most people do not celebrate this day simply because they do not remember it and there are far more important things to think of. But take a moment to think how a little note or a small gift from you to commemorate this kiss might lead to many more kisses in the future.

What about celebrating the first time you were ever intimate with her? What response do you think you might get when you let her know how important that event was in your life?

Just taking the time to send your love is all that really matters

---

Random Anniversaries

Any event of importance is an opportunity for you to commemorate it later. If one year ago today her beloved pet Fluffy died of old age, how impressed and loved will she feel if you recognize that day with a small token of your affection? What about the anniversary of the day she bought her first house, the day she got her new car, the day she had a spiritual breakthrough, the day she got pregnant, or the day she beat cancer. Any important day in her life can be celebrated years later by simply recognizing its existence. She will be impressed and feel loved because those events important in her life are also important in yours.

National Holidays

Easter, Saint Patrick's Day, Thanksgiving, Memorial Day, and the like have no spousal gift obligations associated with them. Thank goodness! However, on Easter, don't let the kids be the only ones to get a basket. On Thanksgiving, if she is preparing food for the family, make sure she gets a little something to show how much you appreciate the work she is doing. National Holidays celebrate events in the nation's history but you can also use them to celebrate events in your history together.

Wife Appreciation Day

What if every year there was one day you went out of your way to shower her with gifts, acts of service, and romance? Imagine how she would respond to you making up a holiday just for her. Imagine what her friends would say to their husbands when your wife tells them of the annual event planned in her honor. Imagine how upset the other husbands will be.

Regardless of the neighborhood fallout, the goal of this new holiday is to show your wife she means the world to you when the world does not require you to do it. It can be far more special than any traditional holiday because you created it solely with her in mind. It might sound crazy but I believe you will find this day to be the most romantic day of the year.

Flower Day

This new day created in her honor is self-explanatory. Pick a day every year and bring her a unique bouquet of flowers. You can either get them from the florist or walk into the fields to pick wildflowers. Where you get them does not matter. The point is to surprise her with flowers on the same day every year. An added attraction can be her lack of anticipation of the event. She can either know about this annual happening or you can keep it a secret and surprise her every year until she figures it out. If she never does, tell her on your fiftieth wedding anniversary.

"Just Because" Day

There is no day on the calendar that cannot be improved by giving her a small token of your affection. Happy Day presents are often the most wonderful because they are a complete surprise. They do not recognize any events and are not anticipated because of some preordained obligation. Happy day presents are given just because you love her and want her to know it.

Note to men

Remember, the more you let her know how much you love her, the more likely you will feel loved in return.

And remember, the non-obligatory gifts do not have to be large impressive items. They are impressive just because they come from the heart.

Chapter 8

Gifts That Send The Wrong Signals

How can gifts send the wrong signals? Is it possible a gift to brighten her day can actually end up having the opposite effect? You bet it can. In fact, you probably faced this unfortunate scenario many times already.

Suppose you decide to give her a gym membership as a happy day present. She has been asking for one for quite some time and you finally made the arrangements. Little did you know, she recently gained six pounds and could not squeeze into her favorite pair of jeans this morning. In disgust, she buried them in the back of her closet where she would not have to look at them. All day she could think of little else. Every time she looked at the clothing she chose to wear, she thought back to this morning's events. Unhappy with her body and therefore herself, she comes through the door at the end of the day barely able to contain her bad mood. And there you stand, holding a gift to blatantly remind her she is way too fat and she better work out before you leave her for a newer, thinner model. Sound familiar?

WARNING!
Avoid any gift if the reaction you are likely to receive is
dependent upon her mood.

It does not matter your intentions were good. It does not matter you had her best interest at heart. It does not matter you are a loving and caring human being who would rather die than hurt her feelings. It does not even matter that she asked you for it. Your timing was off and that is all she needs to make your life a living hell for the next few hours.

There is a long list of gifts straddling the thin line between excellent and appalling. The aforementioned gym membership might be great for a woman who desires to stay fit and asks repeatedly for one. For a woman not in the right frame of mind, you might as well have given her some depilatory cream, a wart remover, and an appointment with a plastic surgeon.

> **You are not going to feel loved as long as she does not feel loved.**

There are even worse signals you can send than the random mood-dependent mistakes. These are the times we make obvious and seemingly intentional gift-giving blunders. For example, say you find your marriage quite loving and equitable. Your only complaint is your spouse should be washing more dishes and perhaps doing more cooking than she has been. For her birthday, you decide to help her by purchasing a new set of dish towels, a couple of designer dish scrubbers, and a very expensive new set of stainless steel pots and pans. What do you think is going to happen when this lovely amiable woman opens up her gifts? It will probably not have the desired response. In fact, there might be far less cooking in both the kitchen and the bedroom for a while.

I admit that I am giving-challenged. I'm generous --- I enjoy giving gifts --- but I lack any creativity in deciding what to give. I honestly thought my wife would be delighted with the beautiful over-and-under shotgun I bought her for our first Christmas together. And when she complained about food sticking to the bottom of our frying pan, I thought that meant she would love a set of Teflon-coated cookware for our anniversary. Fortunately for both of us, she's forgiving, and I learn from my mistakes.

- **Dave Precht**, Editor
Bassmaster Magazine

There are literally hundreds of gift items you can make mistakes with. Anything not adequately reflecting her likes and dislikes is guaranteed to fail. Sexy lingerie might be just the ticket for you, but a real uncomfortable stretch for a conservative woman. And, if she is not going to feel comfortable wearing it, how fun could it really be for you? And what if your significant other loves wearing sexy and provocative outfits? What kind of signal would you send if you bought thick, full coverage outfits to hide the assets she is so proud of?

Remember that gifts should show affection or, at the very least, be something she might actually want to own. Gifts should not reflect shortcomings in the husband / wife dynamic either. That is a door you do not want to open. Think about your own shortcomings and about what she might give you on your next birthday. You might get a "Read This" note on a book entitled, "A Beginners Guide on How to Fulfill a Woman." Simply put, avoid gifts indicating desired behavioral changes. It is a game you cannot win.

Finally, one of the worst signals you could ever send is apathy. There are few things worse for a woman than to sense her man is not thinking about her. If she asks repeatedly for something or makes her desires known about clothing, hobbies, entertainment, and the like, you should do your best to give her what she wants. She should know by your gifts that you are paying attention to her. The worst signal you could possibly send is that you just don't care and are going through the motions.

Sad Fact

The most common gift complaint from women is not receiving a gift at all.

Remember, gift giving does not have to be hard. The fact you are giving a gift in the first place puts you ahead of the game. You only need to pay attention. With a little effort you can send the signal she means everything to you and you will do whatever it takes for her to know it.

Chapter 9

The Street Rose vs. The Flower Shop Rose

Glancing down at his watch to see how late he is, a man leaves work and heads toward home. Making it home for tonight's dinner is extremely important as it is his seventh wedding anniversary and his wife has prepared an elaborate meal. A few blocks from home, he suddenly realizes he did not get her an anniversary gift. He has been so busy lately he did not have time or the foresight to buy a gift for his loving wife in advance. As luck would have it, a red light stops the flow of traffic at an intersection near his home. While waiting for the light to turn, a vender selling individual roses decorated in plastic wrap approaches his car. What great luck? He rolls down the window, spends three dollars on a single long stem red rose and drives off to meet his adoring wife.

Men, don't do it! There is nothing quite so insulting as a last minute afterthought of a gift. The street rose in the above scenario is a horrible idea. Flowers are not the bad idea, just the last minute act of buying one without thought or effort. Remember, women like to feel appreciated. I don't think, "Hey honey, you have been so loving to me lately that I spent fifteen seconds and three whole dollars on you," is the message you are hoping to convey.

> **Take the time to send the message you love her and think about her. She will respond favorably.**

Timing is huge when it comes to how gifts are received. Casual flowers may be just the ticket to brighten a non-descript day but if an event is significant, why not act like it? Take the time to stop at a florist to pick up her favorite bouquet. It does not require large amounts of time but you can bet a special bouquet will be far more appreciated. In this instant a bouquet of flowers from a florist might not be an original or creative idea, but it will never say you are inconsiderate, cheap, and lazy.

Just because street roses are not a great idea in the above scenario, they can be an important addition to your flower-giving repertoire. Consider the following:

A man drives home from golfing with his buddies. It is Saturday afternoon and nothing special is planned at the house. His wife has been out to lunch with her friends and got home about an hour earlier. As the man approaches his home, the same red light stops traffic. Up walks the vendor again and the same single rose is purchased. After entering the house and setting his golf clubs in the hall closet, he gives his wife a kiss and hands her the rose. Surprised, she asks, "What's the occasion." His answer is simply, "No occasion. I just wanted you to know I love you." He gives her another kiss and heads for the shower.

Imagine her thought processes as he disappears from view. At the very least, she will feel more loved than she did even the moment before. Of the two previous scenarios, which man do you think is in a happier relationship?

Almost any gift can send a caring message if the timing is right. All you need to do is ask yourself if the gift will make her feel good about herself or bad about you. Don't make the mistake of thinking you can slip by with convenience. You will spend much more time dealing with the fallout from your actions than you would have spent taking the time to get a more thoughtful and heartfelt gift in the first place.

List two months when there are no gift-giving obligations on you and when she is not expecting anything.

_____   _____

Suggestion: Surprise her with a gift from out of the blue during this time and watch her reaction.

<u>Horror Story #63</u>

Honesty Is The Best Policy

For Christmas one year, Bill saved the best present for last. Proudly, as all the other gifts were opened and set aside, he handed a beautifully wrapped box to his wife Julie and waited with anticipation as she unwrapped it. Inside, Julie discovered a leather bomber jacket. It was clearly expensive and the correct size, but Julie was confused. It was not something she would ever wear and had no idea why Bill gave it to her. Not wanting to hurt his feelings, she offered the words, "I love it," and they went about their day together. During later conversations, Julie learned she had inadvertently said bomber jackets were cool while watching a contemporary war movie. What she meant was, "Guys look cool in bomber jackets." What Bill heard was, "Julie wants one of those."

Although Bill should be praised for listening, he did not quite understand the meaning of her statement. Instead of verifying the information, he trudged forward and purchased what he thought to be a wonderful gift. Sadly, the story does not end there.

About two months later, Bill commented that he never saw Julie in the jacket. Julie thought fast and quickly lied, "Oh Bill, I am so sorry. It was stolen when I was out to lunch with my friends. I did not have the heart to tell you." The truth of the matter was Julie gave it to her friend's twelve-year-old son with instructions never to wear it around Bill. Bill was mildly annoyed but Julie was relieved the ordeal was over. Or was it? One month later, on her birthday, Bill brought out another box. Inside was a new bomber jacket to replace the one Julie loved so much. Firmly entrenched in her lie now, Julie's friends get a big kick out of inviting the two of them to outdoor events in the hopes she will show up wearing her new favorite jacket.

Chapter 10

Pitfalls, Booby Traps, and Landmines

It is well known how men get into trouble continually with the women in their lives. Sometimes, we actually deserve it. Alright, most of the time. But there are those occasional moments when we do exactly as we are asked and still seem to land face down in the mud. It is not our fault and it hardly seems fair, but it does happen. So we must carefully maneuver around the booby traps these so-called loving women create for us.

On my parent's twenty-fifth wedding anniversary, they took a trip to Egypt and a cruise through the Greek Islands. After the vacation was planned my mother made a point of telling my father the trip was so expensive it was to be their only gift to each other. My father saw the inherent logic and agreed. Several times these instructions were repeated to him. Much to his surprise, on the day of their anniversary and onboard the ship in a foreign land, my mother presented him with a diamond-encrusted watch. My father was caught totally unprepared. He had nothing to give her in return. Even though it was her idea in the first place to not give gifts, my mother was clearly hurt. My father purchased a gold necklace for her when the ship docked to rectify the situation but it was not well received. She feigned appreciation, but this time he knew she was not sincere.

If a woman utters the phrase, "I don't want anything," don't believe her! Not only does she want a gift, she is expecting you to give her one. If you fall for this blatant deceit, you will find yourself in a world of emotional hurt. You may have honored her request but you failed to see the bigger picture. She will likely feel deeply hurt at your negligence. Of course it does not make any sense. Of course it is not fair. Women should mean what they say. Tragically, it is not always the case.

When a woman makes a statement like this, she is actually telling you she is not going to help you. She expects you to go out on your own and figure it out. She just doesn't want to sound like she expects you to buy her a present, even though she expects you to buy her a present.

Note to Women

Help your man by giving subtle hints or direct instructions about the gifts you desire. If you lie to conceal your desires, you deserve what you get, or even more to the point, what you do not get.

Other non-truths women utilize to seemingly set traps for us are, "You don't need to get me anything," or, "That is too expensive," or, "Just bring me some flowers and I will be happy." Each of these is fraught with deceit. In fact, you do need to get her something, it may be expensive but she will love it, and you better bring her something in addition to flowers.

And guys, don't fall for the word only. "I only want a new toothbrush and some floor mats for my car," or, "I only want a screen door and a new pair of gloves." Sound familiar? This is her way of saying exactly the same as the previous. She is minimizing the sound of her expectations and leaving it up to you to figure out what she gets.

Not surprisingly, the half-truths women tell are not restricted to the wish list process. Women lie all the time about gifts they receive and dislike. "I love it" is a common utterance. But most statements of this nature are to spare feelings.

I have a drawer in my bedroom reserved for gifts I hate and will never use. I only keep them in case the person comes over and I need to prove I still have them.

- **Camille Farnsworth**

She may be able to fool some friends into thinking she loves their gifts, but your proximity makes it much more difficult for her to conceal her true opinions about the gifts you give her. Don't be surprised if an article of clothing you buy gets returned in favor of one more representative of her desires and you never hear a word about it.

To avoid women's landmines and booby traps, use your common sense and disregard any random statement she makes suggesting she doesn't want or need anything. Of course she does. The simplest way to avoid hurt feelings is by spending a little creative energy thinking up a romantic gift she will be excited to receive. The words "warm" and "fuzzy" should be foremost in your mind. Your gifts should make her feel significant and loved. Disregard anything she says to the contrary.

How Well Do You Know Her?

The answers to any and all questions about your significant other helps to increase your knowledge base. That, in turn, will help your gift giving abilities. The more you know about her, the easier the gift ideas will come to you.

Does she take long baths or short ones? _____

Does she like to entertain or be entertained? _____

Does she prefer crowds or alone time? _____

Does she like to travel or stay close to home? _____

Does she like trying new things? _____

Does a friend own anything she wishes she owned? _____

What is her favorite way to relax? _____

What is her favorite time of day? _____

What is her favorite hobby? _____

What is her favorite climate? _____

Does she prefer the water, the desert, or the mountains?
_____

Does she prefer the indoors or the outdoors? _____

Does she like to read? _____

Does she like to be pampered? _____

Chapter 11

Gifts That Make You Look Stupid

It does not seem fair that gifts carry with them so much baggage. First, they must represent our significant other's wishes and desires. Second, they must be of the appropriate size, shape, timeliness, expense, and quality to signify how important she is. And finally, they must pass through the rigors of the "friend test."

My mother owned a gift shop carrying a large selection of gifts, gourmet foods, Christmas ornaments, cards, toys, novelty items, designer chocolates, and the like. She was always difficult to shop for but after opening her gift store it was impossible to find something new and exciting for her. Everything she liked she either owned already, carried it in the shop, or dad gave it to her. One year, after being thoroughly devoid of Christmas gift ideas, my siblings and I decided to ask her directly what she wanted. Much to our surprise, the only idea she would offer was, "a pink toilet seat." I am not kidding.

Now, although she truly wanted a new pink toilet seat, she raised no dummies. None of us bought it for her. Imagine my mother out to dinner with a couple of her girlfriends after the holiday. What do you think they would say when they discover the gift of a brand new pink toilet seat given by her loving children? What would that gift say about us?

Now something to remember is that your wife or girlfriend is no different. In fact, she will ask for bizarre items you could not have foreseen or imagined. Don't be fooled into giving these things to her.

The one thing you can be sure of is: Women talk. Every one of her girlfriends will most definitely ask about the gifts you gave her. They will inquire how the gifts were wrapped, which gift you gave first, the size, shape, and every other detail. Sadly, this puts one more neurosis into your shopping experience, but it is important for you to remember that friends are brutal. And when it comes to an embarrassing item, your significant other will likely not divulge her desire for the gift in the first place. In fact, she might even get a kick out of telling her friends about it. The only person embarrassed and laughed at is likely to be you.

So what makes an embarrassing or inappropriate gift? It could be anything. A personal hygiene item, cleaning supplies, a toilet seat, a sexual toy of some sort, or any other number of overt items can be inherently filled with gossip potential.

To avoid ridicule and embarrassment, stick to giving romantic gifts.

Now that you know of the abuse you will inevitably take at the hands of her nearest and dearest girlfriends, you are permitted and encouraged to refuse giving her items she asks you for. If you suspect no person in his or her right mind would judge you fairly about giving such an item, don't do it. You may flat out refuse. In fact, tell her directly there is no way she will ever get that particular item as a gift. You can offer to accompany her while she buys it. You can offer to pick one up sometime in January on the way home from work. You could hand her a fist full of cash and insist she go buy it by herself. You are justified in any choice you make. Just do not make the one choice likely to come back to haunt you.

Note to Women

Have a heart. Don't subject your man to embarrassment at the hands
of your friends. He will cause enough of that on his own. If you desire
a potentially embarrassing item, buy it yourself.

Now the good news is the same as the bad news:
Women talk. If you become a loving and thoughtful gift
giver, her girlfriends might find themselves filled with
envy. This is yet another gift you can give your
significant other. How great for her to rattle off the
fantastic well thought-out gifts you presented her. She
can proudly answer all their questions and detail the
superior way you presented these romantic gifts to her.
In fact, the more she talks, the more her friends will
clamor over each gift and how they wish they got the
same items from their husbands.

**You are permitted, and encouraged, to refuse
giving her items she asks you for.**

By the way, my father ended up purchasing the pink
toilet seat for my mother and it was very well received. It
turned out to be a family joke for quite some time. In
fact, because of the constant ribbing before hand, the gift
became a fun item to give. It brought great humor to the
day. Even potentially embarrassing gifts can become
great gifts if the timing and situation are right. But you
can bet your last dollar he gave her a few romantic gifts
as well.

Horror Story #6

Alicia received a set of steak knives for her twenty-ninth birthday. They were nice knives, but they were not romantic. And, to make matters worse, she is a vegetarian. Her boyfriend told her she could cut vegetables with them.

Horror Story #47

Sally received a set of Allen wrenches for Mother's Day from her husband. Apparently, she mentioned she needed them previously for a tiny project. He was obviously listening, he was just not thinking.

Horror Story #61

Diane received a refrigerator for her fourteenth wedding anniversary. In all fairness, it was one of the better refrigerators on the market. If only there were a diamond tennis bracelet in the ice tray.

Horror Story #88

Jennifer received a kitten for the one-year anniversary of their first date. It was a very nice gesture except he forgot she was extremely allergic to them.

Horror Story #93

For Valentine's Day, Karla received a small box of candy, an oil change for her seven-year-old car, and a new ice scraper for her windshield. She only found out later, he got the ice scraper for free when he filled the gas tank of his own car.

Horror Story # 102

Leanne received a gift basket with all her favorite sweets and snacks for her birthday. She also received a bouquet of multi-colored tulips. This would have been a perfect gift except the card he wrote had his ex-girlfriend's name on it, not hers. Oops!

Chapter 12

Differences In Women

This is probably the most important chapter in the book. The concept of every woman being different is one you must grasp before ever venturing into the perilous world of gift giving.

Jerry's wife loves taking long baths. She soaks in a tub for an hour, has soft music playing in the background and a glass of champagne nearby. She reads her books and favorite magazines as she soaks the time away. Many evenings, she just sits quietly taking in the mood and praying no one disturbs her quiet time. She enjoys the gifts of bath soaps and lotions. She loves new mood enhancing CD's and new types of wine or champagne. She loves big comfy bath towels, soft bathrobes, and fuzzy slippers that help her carry the mood of the tub away from the bathroom. She glows after the experience.

Dan's wife finds the bathroom experience to be a necessary evil. It is more of a sporting event for her. The goal is to see how quickly she can shower, shave her legs, and apply whatever creams and lotions that happen to lie around. She rushes from one bathroom task to another and moves on to more important parts of her day. She cannot waste time in the bathroom, as there are bikes to ride, sporting events to go to, and movies to see. Creams, lotions, mood enhancing CD's, bathrobes, and fuzzy slippers are lost on her.

These two women have different likes and dislikes. All women do. What does your sweetheart do in her quiet time? What does she like to do when she is active? How does she spend her day? Does she like being pampered? Does she have any hobbies? Is food something she relishes or is it something to choke down on her way to work? Is she moody? Does she relax by taking long baths or working out in a gym? Does she like quiet time or does she prefer to be surrounded by people twenty-four hours a day? Is she a conservative dresser or does she like flashy clothing? How does her style reflect in her choice of home furnishings and decorations?

Remember, just because a gift worked once, does not mean it will work again. Knowing the unique properties of the woman in your life is the first step toward buying a gift appropriate to her desires. The goal is to let her know you understand her passions and desires and you also have the desire to nourish them.

> **Remember that gifts should show affection or, at the very least, be something she might actually want to own.**

Gift giving is not rocket science. You only need to learn about your sweetheart's possessions, her clothing desires, her taste in food, her preference in pampering techniques, her daily routine, and so on to determine a course of action to take. Cater to her wants and desires and you will do wonderfully.

Chapter 13

E-Gifts: God's Gift To Men

Gentlemen, pay close attention to this chapter. Electronic gifts purchased over the Internet are some of the greatest gifts in the world. Why? Because we don't have to get off our butts and we still look like a hero to our significant others.

The Internet has ushered in a new era of gift giving. Today, we men do not have to leave our office, our homes, or even our couches to buy a gift for our lovely wives and girlfriends. We only need to log onto the Internet, order her a gift, pay with our credit card, and shortly the delivery man shows up at the door with the package. How great is that? And most times we do not even need to wrap our gift. Many websites give the option, most for a small fee, to wrap the packages for us. When the gifts arrive, they are pre-wrapped in the requested style and ready for our lover to open. There is nothing simpler than this. No more shopping in malls. No more gift shops. No more crowds. No more lines. No more last minute trips to the bank to get cash. No more... no more... no more. I love the Internet.

Of course, you can opt to wrap the presents yourself if you want to incorporate a personal touch. You only need to be around to sign for the package and then, at your leisure, find a wrapping paper she might like. It is totally up to you.

Note to Men

Virtually any gift you want can be purchased online. Almost every
store, major chain, and small mom and pop store has a website
for you to view their merchandise.

There is little difficulty finding the gifts you need
online. The sheer number of websites available is like
putting ten million gift stores side by side. For those of
you without Internet experience, don't worry. Once you
get to the Internet, find the "Search" menu and type in
whatever item you are looking for. Be prepared.
Thousands of websites and maybe even millions will turn
up. At this point, you can start clicking on the individual
sites or narrow the focus of your search by adding more
information. Either way, you are moments away from
finding the perfect gift and ending your shopping for the
day.

Recently, I typed in the word "gift" and my search engine came up
with twenty seven million eight hundred thousand websites. I laughed
to myself and logged onto a computer game room to play some
backgammon before returning to my gift search

And don't think the Internet is just good for finding
gifts for the obligatory gift-giving days. Happy day
presents are one of the best uses of this powerful tool.
How excited will your wife be when she opens the door on
a nondescript Wednesday afternoon to find a deliveryman
standing there holding a bouquet of flowers for her? You
don't even need to get off your recliner to see if she likes
them. Moments after reading the card, she will find you.

What if she was in the kitchen and her sterling silver
serving spoon got chopped up by mistake in the garbage
disposal? How do you think she will feel when she opens
the door three days later and a deliveryman hands her a

box from a silver utensil supply store? More importantly, you did not have to make the special trip to get it. Again, you were listening to her problems and took action, but you never had to get off your butt. Sounds like a beautiful thing to me.

> **Although there isn't much danger of this, do not over gift. Give her just enough to keep the gifts unexpected and appreciated.**

Window-shopping over the Internet doesn't feel as tedious to the majority of men either. They can sit in the comfort of their own home and in their own time type random words under the search profile and discover things they never thought of.

Another service the Internet provides is detailed information about any subject. Say you want to get some jewelry but do not know what kind of stone to purchase. The Internet is filled with web pages describing gemstones in every conceivable color, shape, size, and clarity. There is information about jewelry settings and jewelers, and there are scads of websites offering jewelry for sale. A little time spent online can answer all your questions.

> **Always try the Internet first, even if you ultimately choose to buy your gifts from a store.**

On my website, I have made your job even easier. Take a moment to visit www.giftgivinghandbook.com and you will find links to more than one hundred potential gift purchasing sites. These sites range from gourmet foods to athletic gear. You can buy flowers, jewelry, bakery goods, designer chocolates, gift baskets, and home furnishings by clicking from my website to one of the hundreds of others stores and outlets.

The thing to remember is to always go to the Internet first. Even if you choose to buy your gifts from a store, the Internet can provide comparative price shopping and detailed product information before you ever decide to leave the house. This powerful tool can save you loads of time and money.

Chapter 14

The Romantic Gifts

Gentlemen, I cannot stress enough that women do not have a sense of humor when it comes to romance. Since birth, they have been bombarded with images of the perfect wedding, the fairy tale romance, the magical prince on his white horse, and growing old with the man of their dreams. These are ingrained images of a very powerful nature. Although you have no possibility of living up to them, you can give her brief moments of brilliance to fulfill her dreams, albeit temporarily.

Jewelry

When interviewing women, the first question I always asked was, "What is the most romantic gift you ever received?" The second question was, "What kind of gift would you most like to receive?" For more than three quarters of the women, the answer to both questions had something to do with jewelry. They talked about diamonds, rubies, emeralds, and other precious stones. They talked about rings, necklaces, and tennis bracelets. They varied in their desires but not in their topic.

You can get links added or taken out of a good bracelet. Add more diamonds if it is too small.

- Elizabeth O'Brien

Although often expensive, the gift of jewelry carries with it a great deal of sentiment. When you truly want your significant other to know how much she means to you, a gift of precious stones and metals usually does the trick.

Flowers

Another of the romantic favorites, flowers come in all shapes and colors. They are quite easy to acquire and relatively inexpensive. And yet, they say so much. Most women love to get flowers. I'm not sure which they like more: The flowers themselves or the fact you think enough about them to get the flowers in the first place. Do yourself a huge favor and give her flowers regularly. They are great for special occasions and as an everyday reminder of your love for her. Send them to her office or bring them home with you. Even if buying a different gift altogether, a vase of flowers is a beautiful addition and can only serve to make her feel that much more special.

Never underestimate the power of a flower

Candy & Sweets

Many people use candy in addition to flowers or as a stand-alone gift idea. Gourmet chocolates and designer sweets might be just the thing to brighten her day. Take time to figure out when a gift of candy might make her feel appreciated. She might end up sweeter than the gift.

Perfume

Now this is an interesting item. When interviewing, I discovered many younger women thought perfume was immensely romantic. In fact, one group of three women under twenty-five years of age answered, "perfume," in unison when asked what romantic gift they would like to receive from a man. Many of the older women, however, already knew what fragrances they liked and did not vary much from that particular scent. My only suggestion might be to give it a shot and see how it turns out. If you are unsure, ask her if she likes trying new scents. If not, stick to some of the other styles of romantic gifts. But if you do try to surprise her with a new fragrance, consider giving her flowers in tandem to make sure she feels the romance even if the perfume doesn't work for her.

Vacations

Trips to special places can often be the most romantic gifts you ever give her. Many women feel trapped in their ordinary lives and nothing changes their attitude like a nice romantic getaway. Try surprising your sweetheart with a quick jaunt away from home or an all-inclusive vacation package. If surprises are not her thing, have her give you a list of her most desirable travel destinations and spend some time planning the trip with her.

The goal is to get her away from her normal life and spend some much-needed quality time together. Maybe you will rekindle the flame that brought you together in the first place. There is nothing like warm ocean breezes, long walks on the beach, and drinks in the cabana to get the passions flowing again.

Experiences

Much like vacations, new experiences can be very romantic. A spa day for two, a night at the theatre, hiking up to natural hot springs in the mountains, and many other experiences can arouse her senses. Besides the fun nature of these new experiences, when shared they have the added attraction of bringing the two of you closer together.

Personal Gifts

What is she passionate about? What are the truly important things in her life? If family is one of her passions, secretly have a family portrait made from a nearby artist. Maybe it is just the two of you right now. Try having a portrait made from her favorite romantic photograph. On Valentine's Day, have her unwrap this secret gift along with some flowers and a card telling her how you feel about her. Odds are she will beam with warmth as she absorbs your love and caring.

What three things is she most passionate about?

_____ _____ _____

What if she has been looking for a missing piece to one of her collections for fifteen years? How romantic will it be for her to open up a gift and discover you spent great deals of time finding it for her? What if something of great rarity and sentimental value got lost or broken? You may get the same response by finding and replacing that very same item.

Personal gifts refer to things she considers special. Other people might not regard them as romantic, but she will. Again, the romance can come from the gift itself but more likely will come from the fact you were thinking about her and her desires. A loving and caring attitude can be the most romantic gift of all.

Chapter 15

She Doesn't Need More Stuff, Just Better Stuff

How old is your refrigerator? How about your furniture, your VCR, your pots and pans, your bedspreads, or your clothing? My guess is you have quite a few items you would not mind replacing with new and improved models. Odds are, she could use some newer stuff as well.

The secret to giving good gifts is finding the right idea. Fortunately for the inept man, there are those gift ideas utilizing no imagination, no creativity, and very few observational skills. When gift giving time rolls around, he can sit in each room of her house with a notepad and pencil and within seconds have a complete list of items needing replaced. This makes shopping so much easier. All he needs to do is buy an item or two from his list, add one romantic gift, and his job is done.

Note to Women

As gift time approaches, don't be shy. If you have an item needing
replaced, let him know about it. He will be grateful he did not
have to come up with an idea on his own.

Although these gifts cater wonderfully to the inept man's sensibilities, don't be lulled into thinking you can get away with replacing a couple of items and expect her to fall into your arms feeling all warm and fuzzy. Not a chance. Replacements are usually filler gifts to be given in conjunction with other offerings. Surely by now you are getting a sense that warm and fuzzy feelings only come from romantic items, personal items, or objects she has been desperately seeking and unable to find or afford.

WARNING!

Many items women own have sentimental value. Be careful not to replace an item with emotions attached to it. If she cares about you, she will feel obligated to display the gift you purchased and dispose of the item she truly loved.

If somehow you do make the mistake of replacing a sentimental item, let her off the hook. If she liked the older, familiar item better or was emotionally attached to it, tell her she can take yours back and you will buy her something else. She will love you all the more for understanding.

List a dozen things she owns which could be improved or replaced.

_____ _____ _____

_____ _____ _____

_____ _____ _____

_____ _____ _____

Chapter 16

Give Her A Break; She Deserves It

What does your wife do for a living? Is she a housewife? Do you have kids? Is she a career woman? Regardless of her occupation, odds are she works very hard. Why not ask yourself if she would rather have a gift you purchase in a store that sits around gathering dust or something to help her with her work, her stress, her mood, or her general well being?

Gifts can be anything, but rarely are they more appreciated than when they really ease her burdens. If your significant other spends her days cooking and cleaning for you and the kids, try giving her something she will truly enjoy. Hire a maid for a week. If you don't have lots of expendable dollars, hire her for one day. Have the newly employed maid take over all the cleaning and cooking so your wife can do anything she wants to for that day. It is a day for her to play. She might lie by a lake somewhere reading a book. She might go for a long walk and get some much-needed outdoor time. She might hook up with her girlfriends for a long overdue get-together lunch. Regardless what she does with her time, you will likely be the dominant force in her heart and mind.

> **What are her two least favorite chores?**
>
> _____
>
> _____

What happens when your wife is stressed to her breaking point? A great gift here might be a spa day. First, it gets her out of the house. This is great for her and probably your peace of mind too. Second, she gets some much needed pampering. Day spas are very easy to find and soothing to the nerves. Even if your significant other is a delight to be around and shows no signs of stress, give her this gift every once in a while anyway. Women adore these spas for the facials, steam baths, hot tubs, sea salt rubdowns, mudpacks, pedicures, manicures, and massages. Pampering is the name of the game. Whether stressed or not going in, chances are she will be relaxed and calm coming out. Spa days are truly one of the great gifts men can bestow on the women in their lives. If for no other reason than showing her how much you love her, the pampering she gets at a day spa enhances the way she feels about herself and you.

Note to Men

Give her a spa day for two or convince the husband of her best friend
to give a spa day to his wife also. The women can go together and
it will enhance the experience for both of them.

If you have children and she is the main caregiver, call in a favor from some friends. Secretly trade babysitting duties with them. Tell your friends you will watch their children one weekend if they watch yours. Surprise your wife by giving her a special day away from the kids.

If she hates washing clothing, pack them and take them to a professional laundry once in a while. Go on a picnic instead of doing domestic tasks. If she works a nine to five job, secretly arrange a day off with her boss and surprise her by picking her up at the office and whisking her out of there. If she doesn't seem to have enough time to see her friends, surprise her by arranging a lunch with all of them for her. Anything you can do to make her life easier shows her how much you care and just as important, how much you listen.

Find original and exciting ideas to give her a break from the mundane. If she drives the kids to school every day but finds her old car frustrating or just plain boring, rent her a convertible sports car for the day. After dropping the kids off at school, have her pick you up at the office and take you to lunch. It may sound silly, but she may drop you off after eating lunch and head for the open road. Who knows? A day behind the wheel with the top down might be just the thing she needs to relax and feel special.

There are so many ways to give her the break she needs. Just ask yourself what chore she performs on a day-to-day or week-to-week basis that she would rather not do. Find a way to have someone else take over those tasks. If you can't think of anything, ask her? She will be more than happy to let you know the things she does not like doing and will likely be pleased you are interested enough to ask in the first place.

More Questions

Again, the more information you have, the easier gift buying becomes.

What is her favorite smell? _____

What is her favorite sound? _____

Is her personality conservative or flashy? _____

Is her clothing conservative or flashy? _____

Is she very particular about her clothing? _____

What does she do in her quiet time? _____

What does she do for a living? _____

Is food something she relishes or just something to choke down on her way to work? _____

What are her hobbies? _____   _____

Does she enjoy spending great deals of time at home? _____

What is her favorite room in the house? _____

Is she a traditional or contemporary person? _____

Chapter 17

It Is The Little Things That Count

Small gestures to show you listen to her and understand her needs can be very rewarding to your significant other. If she complains that the rain on her windshield makes it impossible for her to see clearly, replace her wiper blades. If she shreds meat and bread instead of cutting it cleanly, buy her a new set of knives or sharpen the knives she already has. If her back is hurting, give her a massage or buy her an ergonomic chair. Fix a broken cabinet door or hire someone to do it for you. If her favorite belt does not fit her anymore, punch another hole in the leather (with her permission of course) to make it possible for her to wear again. Show her you are listening to her problems and are actively interested in making her life more enjoyable.

I am not trying to suggest women will swoon over every little thing you do for them. In fact, the simple task of replacing a broken lock is insignificant. However, taking the opportunity to show her you think about her needs is not. Fixing little problems may not be life changing, but it surely raises your stock a little.

The thing that sets some men apart from all the others is their willingness to help out with the little things. Carrying groceries in from the car, replacing a broken lock, and fixing a flat tire may not seem like much, but it sure shows me he cares.

- Candice Jenkins

And don't think little acts of kindness are restricted to things that stop working. There are many opportunities to do little things for her that add joy to her life. If she likes birds, install a birdfeeder outside her bedroom window or on her patio. Fill it with birdseed and treat her to constant companionship as the birds flock to their food. If she loves music, program a CD with all her favorite tracks and put it in her car stereo for her next long drive.

Buy her massaging gel cushions for her hiking boots, connect her stereo wires, re-tile the bathroom floor, earthquake proof her house, or stack a cord of wood for her. There are virtually hundreds of little anticipatory things you can do for her. In fact, many of the women interviewed indicated they would rather have a multitude of little things done for them instead of

List five things she has been complaining about lately.

_____

_____

_____

_____

_____

receiving the occasional big gift. Don't miss out on this opportunity to let her know how much you care.

There is, however, one small act of kindness she will likely appreciate above all others. Remember that old faded athletic shirt you own with the holes and the big stain on the side? You know, the one she hates with a passion. Give it to her and let her destroy it. That goes for your old comfy leather chair not matching anything she owns, the left over sporting equipment cluttering up the garage, and any other items she deems worthless and gaudy. It is time to let go of your single past where your broken and ugly possessions carry sentimental value. Oddly enough, her destruction of these items will make her feel even better about you.

There is happiness in any relationship where the partners make a point of addressing each other's needs. You can go a long way toward making your significant other feel loved and secure by not passing over the simple opportunities.

Horror Story #26

A Tasteful Gift

While sitting at the Pai Gow tables in Las Vegas, I struck up a conversation with a delightful woman in her fifties. She asked what I did for a living and when I told her the subject matter of this book, she let out a belly laugh to light up the room. She said, "Let me know when you finish it. I have the perfect man to give one too." She went on to tell me how her ex-husband, who she is still good friends with, gave her a gallon of teriyaki sauce for their tenth wedding anniversary. It was unfortunately her only gift for that day. She never quite understood it, but now finds it tremendously funny.

Supposedly, her ex-husband never remarried. Imagine that.

Chapter 18

She Has Never Done That Before

So, you have no clear-cut idea what she wears. You have no idea what furniture goes nicely in her house. You have no idea what novelty items she likes, what food she eats, what services you can perform for her, or what hobbies she is into. Basically, you have not been paying any attention for the last three years. Now it is getting close to a special gift-giving day and you are drawing a blank. What do you do now? Don't panic, we've all been there.

Why not provide her with an adventure and a life full of memories? Gifts of "experiences" can be some of the most satisfying gifts you ever give your sweetheart. Most people have something they would like to accomplish in their life before they die but never got around to doing it. This is a perfect opportunity for you to help fulfill one of her dreams.

And new experiences do not have to be as substantial as a vacation abroad. They can be anything. Later in this book, in the chapter

---

List five things she has always wanted to try

_____

_____

_____

_____

_____

entitled *Three Thousand Gift Ideas,* there are hundreds of possible new experience ideas for the both of you. Take her on a train ride to the wine country of California or the New England countryside. Take her bungee jumping, hot air ballooning, or to Las Vegas. Get involved in a pottery class or dancing lessons. There are thousands of new experiences out there for the trying. Anything she has never experienced before is a candidate for this gift giving opportunity.

> **Adventures do not have to be costly. Just use your imagination and let the memory making begin.**

Of course, all women are different and the dreams of some are much more conservative than the dreams of others. That is the beauty of this gift genre. It can be tailored to fit any woman's spirit. If she hates heights, don't take her for a helicopter ride. If she doesn't like to travel, do something local. Find a new experience fitting her specific adventurous nature. Take a ballroom dance class with her at the local college. Take her to a blueberry farm to pick her own fruit. My mother took us to pick our own blueberries, strawberries, and apples and we loved it. If your sweetheart has never tried it before, maybe she will get a kick out of it. Or maybe she would prefer going to a professional sporting event or the theatre.

If your honey is ultra adventurous, take her for a fighter jet ride, take her to play paintball, or take her spelunking. She may enjoy going on safari, swimming with the dolphins, scuba diving, or shooting skeet. There are hundreds of high-octane experiences out there just waiting for her.

Even if the experience fails miserably and she doesn't enjoy the adventure, there might be some residual entertainment for her. Ever hear a story like this:

Well, four years ago Bob got the great idea to cut down our own Christmas tree. We walked around blindly in three feet of snow for hours and finally found a decent one. By then, my feet were numb, my lips were blue, and I wanted to use the axe on him instead of the tree. But calmer heads prevailed and Bob cut it down without killing himself. Anyway, he started dragging it back to the car. That left me to carry the huge axe and about thirty pounds of rope. I was never so cold in my life. Bob must have sensed this was not all he built it up to be and kept asking me if I was having fun. I just looked at him like he was crazy. By the time we got back to the car, all the needles had been pulled off from dragging the tree what seemed to be twenty miles. We stood it up next to the car and it looked like some demented cartoon Christmas tree. It was so sad. Bob tied it to the hood of the car anyway. It died after a week and we had to buy another one from a tree lot around the corner.

Even if she hates the entire experience, she will get great pleasure out of embarrassing you by telling the story over and over to your friends. And realistically, that might be a bigger gift to her than the adventure ever could have been. Just remember that a gift of experience is not just a one-time gift. Fun or not, the memories will last a lifetime.

And don't panic if you are without lots of extra money. Adventures and gifts of experience don't have to be costly. There are hundreds of new adventures requiring very little money at all. There are long hikes in local forests, camping trips, a drive to the mountains to see snow for the first time, horseback riding, or spending time in an Indian sweat lodge. Anything is possible. Money is not a prerequisite for this type of gift. Just use your imagination and let the memory making begin.

Chapter 19

Hit The Road: Gifts of Travel

Your loving wife has been taking care of your children, working the same job for years, and tending to most of your needs. Living in the same house for what seems like forever, her daily routine is set in stone. Her furniture has not been replaced in a decade and she has been driving the same car through two engines and three sets of tires. No offense to you, but she must be bored to tears by now. If this sounds familiar, and even if it doesn't, get her out of town. Either with or without you, she needs and deserves a vacation.

Last year, my friend Daniel told me he didn't know where to take his wife for vacation and wondered if I had any ideas. I simply asked about her interests. He told me she collects antique dollhouses, takes dance and yoga classes, and loves entertaining her friends with wine and cheese parties. I asked if she had ever been to Napa Valley in California to visit the wineries. His words to me were, "She always wanted to go to Napa but never had the opportunity." I just looked at him smugly. A sheepish grin appeared on his face as he turned to walk away from me.

Gifts of travel coincide with personal interests or can be a great opportunity for experimentation. Like other experiences, travel runs the gamut from tame to adventurous. A canoe ride through the Everglades would mesmerize some women while

> **What is her favorite season?**
>
> _____

a five star hotel on the French Riviera would excite others. Regardless of the destination, get her out of the house and into a new environment.

What if she has always dreamed of traveling to Europe? Try handing her a gift basket with some Dutch cheese, Belgian chocolates, French bread, German strudel, and a couple of airline tickets to her most desired travel destinations. Imagine her reaction when she realizes she is about to fulfill a lifelong dream. In addition, a gift like this lasts a tremendously long time. First, it carries with it the wonderful anticipation for several weeks before the trip begins. Then, she has the trip itself. And finally, she has the lasting memories of the vacation of a lifetime.

If you don't know where to start when planning a vacation, ask her. Virtually everyone has a most wanted list when it comes to travel destinations.

When it came to planning travel, my parents wrote down their "Dream Vacation" lists independently of each other. Then, they put the lists together and tried to incorporate both lists into one trip. By doing this, they found themselves in several exotic locations and on interesting vacations other people would never have discovered.

If she comes up blank when you ask her about travel wishes, get yourself to the local bookstore. There are numerous shelves of vacation ideas, both local and long distance. Travel is big business and travel books are abundant. I stopped by my local bookstore and within seconds had twenty great travel ideas within a one-hour drive of my home. I promise you, fifteen minutes in the travel section of any bookstore will give you ideas to last years. Even if you know where you want to go, a book on the destination is a great companion gift. She can read all about the destination and the best places to visit while she travels or before she even leaves the house.

Note to Men

Try a grand experiment. Buy a random book on travel and do whatever it says. You might find yourselves in unique and exciting new situations.

If for whatever reason you cannot find anything at the bookstore, get online. The Internet is the modern world's best source of easily accessible information. Go to your web browser and type in "Resorts," "Festivals," "Tourism," "National Parks," or "Travel Destinations," and see how many websites come up for you. As a keyword for your search, use any hobby or passion your wife enjoys. Thousands of detailed sites, devoted to your topic, will appear to help you with more information than you could possibly desire.

Buy a map and a book on your travel destination to accompany all travel. She might be impressed at your foresight.

While researching this book, I did an Internet search on festivals. Did you know there are more than twenty thousand festivals worldwide? There are festivals on just about any subject you can imagine. There are crab festivals, fireworks festivals, Viking festivals, zoo festivals, and bathtub races. There are sports festivals, rattlesnake festivals, holiday festivals, civil war festivals, and even tattoo festivals. There are music festivals, flower festivals, fruit festivals, dance festivals, festivals celebrating celebrities and festivals celebrating history. Imagine the number of festivals held in your state you are not currently up to speed on. If you are looking for original travel ideas, plan a vacation or even a day trip around the fun and quirky festivals she might be interested in.

If your sweetheart is a resort-type person, that's no problem. There are tens of thousands of resorts worldwide. Tourism is such a large business that just about every city in every country creates resort environments to attract your vacation dollars. The only difficulty is narrowing the search to the resorts that best suit her desires. The following represent just some of the adventurous possibilities.

Which resorts would she be most interested in?

☐ Beach	☐ Hunting	☐ Golf
☐ Lakeside	☐ Safari	☐ Ski
☐ Mountain	☐ Fishing	☐ Riding
☐ Desert	☐ Wilderness	☐ Gambling
☐ Tropical	☐ Island	☐ Castle
☐ Spa	☐ Nude	☐ Recreational
☐ National Park	☐ International	Vehicle
☐ Scuba	☐ Bed & Breakfast	☐ Cruise Liners

The Internet is a great source of information here too. All you need are a few clicks from your mouse and you will have a list of resorts meeting whatever criteria you seek, in whatever country you want.

If you don't have much money, travel can still be the ticket for you. Go on a day-trip to a nearby town or spend some time sightseeing at a National Park.

Important Tip

Sit down with a travel agent before planning your trip. She is a travel professional, has tons of travel information at her disposal, and is trained to help plan your trip. She is also knowledgeable about promotions, package deals, and can search for any travel ideas to fit your specific budget. Don't dismiss this valuable information source.

The important thing is to get her out of her familiar surroundings and into interesting new environments. The only thing you need to do is find out what kind of travel interests her. The more you know about her, the more rewarding the trip will be.

Which States would she most like to visit?

☐ Alabama	☐ Louisiana	☐ Ohio
☐ Alaska	☐ Maine	☐ Oklahoma
☐ Arizona	☐ Maryland	☐ Oregon
☐ Arkansas	☐ Massachusetts	☐ Pennsylvania
☐ California	☐ Michigan	☐ Rhode Island
☐ Colorado	☐ Minnesota	☐ South Carolina
☐ Connecticut	☐ Mississippi	☐ South Dakota
☐ Delaware	☐ Missouri	☐ Tennessee
☐ Florida	☐ Montana	☐ Texas
☐ Georgia	☐ Nebraska	☐ Utah
☐ Hawaii	☐ Nevada	☐ Vermont
☐ Idaho	☐ New Hampshire	☐ Virginia
☐ Illinois	☐ New Jersey	☐ Washington
☐ Indiana	☐ New Mexico	☐ West Virginia
☐ Iowa	☐ New York	☐ Wisconsin
☐ Kansas	☐ North Carolina	☐ Wyoming
☐ Kentucky	☐ North Dakota	

Which Countries would she most like to visit?

Europe

- ☐ Albania
- ☐ Andorra
- ☐ Austria
- ☐ Belarus
- ☐ Belgium
- ☐ Bosnia-Herzegovina
- ☐ Bulgaria
- ☐ Canary Islands
- ☐ Croatia
- ☐ Cyprus
- ☐ Czech republic
- ☐ Denmark
- ☐ England
- ☐ Estonia
- ☐ Faeroe Islands
- ☐ Finland
- ☐ France
- ☐ Georgia
- ☐ Germany
- ☐ Greece
- ☐ Greenland
- ☐ Holy See
- ☐ Hungary
- ☐ Iceland
- ☐ Ireland
- ☐ Italy
- ☐ Latvia
- ☐ Liechtenstein
- ☐ Lithuania
- ☐ Luxembourg
- ☐ Macedonia
- ☐ Malta
- ☐ Moldova
- ☐ Monaco
- ☐ Netherlands
- ☐ Norway
- ☐ Poland
- ☐ Portugal
- ☐ Romania
- ☐ Scotland
- ☐ Slovakia
- ☐ Slovenia
- ☐ Spain
- ☐ Sweden
- ☐ Switzerland
- ☐ Ukraine
- ☐ Wales

Africa

- ☐ Algeria
- ☐ Angola
- ☐ Benin
- ☐ Botswana
- ☐ Burkina Faso
- ☐ Burundi
- ☐ Cameroon
- ☐ Cape Verde
- ☐ Central African Republic
- ☐ Chad
- ☐ Comoros
- ☐ Congo DR
- ☐ Congo Rep.
- ☐ Cote D'Ivoire
- ☐ Djibouti
- ☐ Egypt
- ☐ Equatorial Guinea
- ☐ Eritrea
- ☐ Ethiopia
- ☐ Gabon
- ☐ Gambia
- ☐ Ghana
- ☐ Guinea Bissau
- ☐ Kenya
- ☐ Lesotho
- ☐ Liberia
- ☐ Libya
- ☐ Madagascar
- ☐ Malawi
- ☐ Mali
- ☐ Mauritania
- ☐ Mauritius
- ☐ Mayotte
- ☐ Morocco
- ☐ Mozambique
- ☐ Namibia
- ☐ Niger
- ☐ Nigeria
- ☐ Reunion
- ☐ Rwanda
- ☐ Sao Tome & Principe
- ☐ Senegal
- ☐ Seychelles
- ☐ Sierra Leone
- ☐ Somalia

- ☐ South Africa
- ☐ Sudan
- ☐ Swaziland
- ☐ Tanzania
- ☐ Togo
- ☐ Tunisia
- ☐ Uganda
- ☐ Zambia
- ☐ Zimbabwe

Asia

- ☐ Armenia
- ☐ Azerbaijan
- ☐ Bangladesh
- ☐ Bhutan
- ☐ Brunei
- ☐ Cambodia
- ☐ China
- ☐ East Timor
- ☐ Georgia
- ☐ Hong Kong
- ☐ India
- ☐ Indonesia
- ☐ Japan
- ☐ Kazakhstan
- ☐ Kyrgyz Stan
- ☐ Laos
- ☐ Malaysia
- ☐ Maldives
- ☐ Mongolia
- ☐ Myanmar
- ☐ Nepal
- ☐ North Korea
- ☐ Pakistan
- ☐ Philippines
- ☐ Russian Federation
- ☐ Singapore
- ☐ South Korea
- ☐ Sri Lanka
- ☐ Taiwan
- ☐ Tajikistan
- ☐ Thailand
- ☐ Turkmenistan
- ☐ Tibet
- ☐ Uzbekistan
- ☐ Vietnam

Middle East

- ☐ Afghanistan
- ☐ Bahrain
- ☐ Iran
- ☐ Iraq
- ☐ Israel
- ☐ Jordan
- ☐ Kuwait
- ☐ Lebanon
- ☐ Oman
- ☐ Qatar
- ☐ Saudi Arabia
- ☐ Syria
- ☐ Turkey
- ☐ United Arab Emirates
- ☐ Yemen

Australia

- ☐ American Samoa
- ☐ Australia
- ☐ Cook Islands
- ☐ Fiji
- ☐ French Polynesia
- ☐ Guam
- ☐ Kiribati
- ☐ Marshall Islands
- ☐ Micronesia
- ☐ Nauru
- ☐ New Caledonia
- ☐ New Zealand
- ☐ Palau
- ☐ Papua New Guinea
- ☐ Pitcairn Island
- ☐ Samoa
- ☐ Solomon Islands
- ☐ Tonga
- ☐ Tuvalu
- ☐ Vanuatu

Central & South America

- Argentina
- Belize
- Bolivia
- Brazil
- Chile
- Colombia
- Costa Rica
- Ecuador
- El Salvador
- Falkland Islands
- French Guiana
- Guatemala
- Guyana
- Honduras
- Nicaragua
- Panama
- Paraguay
- Peru
- Suriname
- Uruguay
- Venezuela

North America & Mexico

- Antigua
- Aruba
- Bahamas
- Barbados
- Bermuda
- Bonaire
- British Virgin Islands
- Canada
- Cayman Islands
- Cuba
- Curacao
- Dominica
- Dominican Republic
- Grenada
- Guadeloupe
- Haiti
- Jamaica
- Martinique
- Mexico
- Montserrat
- Puerto Rico
- Trinidad & Tobago
- Turks & Caicos Islands
- United States of America
- United States Virgin Island

A final word with regard to travel is to discover everything around your own home first. Friends who lived in Los Angeles for more than twenty years are still mesmerized by how much they have not seen and done. Now, Los Angeles may be bigger than most cities, but there are undoubtedly many unique and undiscovered places of interest near your hometown. Once you have exhausted everything local, travel within the Continental United States and stay with relatives or friends to stretch vacation dollars. The only thing that really matters is getting her out of the house and taking the time to explore. She will likely be very pleased about the memories you create together.

Chapter 20

Gifts To Arouse The Senses

Every one of the five senses; sight, sound, smell, taste, and touch give a unique opportunity for gift giving. The goal is to find those things you can give and do for her to touch the basic parts of her spirit.

It is Friday evening. An exhausted woman staggers through the door after a long workweek. As she enters the room, she sees the lights are low and candles are lit. A glass of wine sits on the table next to a note reading, "The kids are spending the night at a friend's house and I am in the bathroom. Bring the wine." Interested, but leery of his intentions, she walks into the bathroom to see what her husband is up to. Surprisingly, he is fully dressed and holding a plate of sliced mango, strawberries, and apples (her favorite fruits.) Her preferred jazz music plays softly from the stereo and a hint of vanilla permeates the room from the burning wicks of the scented candles. Steam rises from beneath the bubbles in the bathtub. He smiles and says, "Take a bath and don't come out until you feel relaxed and happy. I'll be waiting to give you a massage. I know you had a tough week and this is my way to help you unwind."

In this one event, the man touched every one of her senses. He had her favorite music playing to help her sense of Sound. He had wine and her favorite fruits for Taste. Lights were dimmed and candles lit to visually please her. The candles were scented to move her sense of Smell and the bath made her feel all warm and fuzzy,

What are her favorite Stores?
_____
_____
_____

obviously affecting her sense of Touch. Imagine how nice this would feel to almost any woman at almost any time. It can be a tremendous stress reliever for those times she has a rough week or it could be the start of a romantic evening for two. Why not try it with your wife and see how she feels afterward.

The goal is to present her with gifts to make her senses come alive. To arouse her sense of Sight, find wonderful things for her to look at. Hang a prism in a sunny window to cast rainbows all over the room or buy a piece of artwork she has been admiring. Paint her living space or plant a flower garden for her. Make her environment visually breathtaking for her. Maybe even buy her some new jewelry. A new diamond tennis bracelet might be a gift she is powerless to take her eyes off of.

To arouse her sense of Sound, buy a music box, wind chimes, or her favorite CD. Install a water garden outside her bedroom window so the sounds of falling water permeate her room at night. At the very least, buy some breathing aids or snoring spray to make her night more restful by freeing her of your noise pollution.

For Taste, find her favorite fruits, candies, and foods. Experiment with designer cookies, brownies, and other sweets. Buy her gourmet chocolates or throw a chocolate fondue party. Take her for a night on the town to her favorite restaurant followed by a trip to her favorite dessert shop.

For Touch, massages of all kinds, warm slippers, and soft fabrics might enhance her mood. A spa day to help her relax can do wonders for her spirit. Buy a warm full-length bathrobe or some big fluffy towels. A silk nightshirt might be a tremendous comfort as she lounges in the evening reading her book.

For Smell, find her favorite scented candles, potpourri, bath oils, and incense. Perfumes and body sprays are always a welcome gift. Maybe even buy her the "new car smell in a can" to enhance her daily driving experience.

You should have fun with this chapter. You can stick to one sensory theme or plan a night giving a gift from each of the five sensory categories. Just take some time to personalize the gifts to match her unique nature and you will find great deals of gift-giving success. With a little creativity, you can enhance a good mood or perhaps even change a bad one.

Clothing Sizes

First, you must know that clothing sizes are all messed up. Some stores have sizes like 2,3, 4, and so on. Others have sizes like small, medium, and large, etc. Is your wife an "8" and a "medium," or, is she an "8" and a "small?" Where does she carry her weight? In her hips, her upper body, her butt, or her legs? Is she petite? Just know that sometimes you will be required to get "Separates." You might have to get a small top and medium bottoms. And just when you think you have it figured out... A size "6" in one store is likely to be different than a size "6" in a different store.

Be this as it may, the answers to the following questions can give you a general guideline to work with.

What is her blouse size?   ☐ 1 ☐ 2 ☐ 3 ☐ 4 ☐ 5 ☐ 6 ☐ 7 ☐ 8 ☐ 9
    ☐ 10 ☐ 11 ☐ 12 ☐ 13 ☐ 14 ☐ other___
    ☐ S ☐ M ☐ L ☐ XL ☐ XXL

What is her pants size?   ☐ 1 ☐ 2 ☐ 3 ☐ 4 ☐ 5 ☐ 6 ☐ 7 ☐ 8 ☐ 9
    ☐ 10 ☐ 11 ☐ 12 ☐ 13 ☐ 14 ☐ other___
    ☐ S ☐ M ☐ L ☐ XL ☐ XXL

What is her dress size?   ☐ 1 ☐ 2 ☐ 3 ☐ 4 ☐ 5 ☐ 6 ☐ 7 ☐ 8 ☐ 9
    ☐ 10 ☐ 11 ☐ 12 ☐ 13 ☐ 14 ☐ other___
    ☐ S ☐ M ☐ L ☐ XL ☐ XXL

What is her jacket size? _____   What is her shoe size? _____

What is her belt size? _____   What is her hat size? _____

What is her bra / cup size? _____   What is her glove size? _____

What is her underwear size? _____

Chapter 21

Gifts During Tragedies

Tragedies befall everyone. It seems life is filled with physical and emotional potholes. Sure you can avoid them for a while, but no person escapes completely. When tragedies happen, genuine friends and loved ones rally to help. How nice is it when people recognize your pain? You can be sure it is no different for her. This can be one of the smartest times to give her a gift.

What if your wife recently lost her eighty-three year old grandmother whom she dearly loved? Alternating between emptiness and pain, she cannot quite let her grandmother go. What if one day you wrap a blanket around her grieving shoulders, only for her to realize it is the quilt belonging to that very same grandmother? Unbeknownst to her, you recognized her grief and called her grandfather. You explained the pain she was going through and had her grandfather ship you an item she would most relate to. This small gift might remind her of the love she still has in this world and could go a long way toward helping her through her loss. And how do you think this gesture would make her feel about you?

> **Giving a gift may not fix her pain, but it sure lets her know you understand it.**

What if her father was fading due to old age and needed full time care in a nursing home? Previously, she told you about the endless games of Chess she and her dad played while rambling on for hours and how much she missed his company. What do you think she would say if you asked the family for the Chess Set and presented it to her when she was feeling blue? You see, in circumstances like this, the goal is not to fix her problem but to let her know you understand it and perhaps even share it.

> **A loving and caring attitude can be the greatest gift of all**

Humor is not out of the question in many semi-tragic situations either. What if she breaks her leg while skiing? More than likely she will be rather unhappy about losing vacation time, let alone the discomfort, embarrassment, and pain she must be feeling. What would happen if you came through the door with a bottle of wine, a long back scratcher for her to use on the inevitable itch inside her leg cast, and a book entitled, "Skiing Basics for Simpletons?" She may feign anger, but odds are she will appreciate you for understanding her pain and trying to help her through it. She will also get mileage out of it for years as she tells the story of your unsympathetic attitude over and over to her friends.

The goal with this type of giving is to help her through a painful point in her life. Not to suggest a little token of affection will remove her pain but it sure helps to know other people understand what she is going through. Sometimes that can be as important to her as anything else you could possibly do.

Chapter 22

Stealth Gifts

A man comes home on his seventh anniversary carrying an ornately wrapped gift. His loving wife meets him at the door with a kiss. They move into the living room where he hands her the gift and takes off his coat. Anxiously she looks at the beautiful bow and decorative wrapping, waiting for his permission to open the box. He smiles and gives her the go-ahead. Slowly but deliberately she tears the wrapping from the package and opens the box. Inside sits the newest model toilet plunger the store had in stock.

What kind of guy would be so stupid? Imagine the confusion his wife must be experiencing.

> **Warm and fuzzy feelings only come from romantic items, personal items, or objects she has been desperately seeking and unable to afford**

Now, the same man and woman, but a different scenario: He walks through the door on a non-descript Tuesday afternoon and into the kitchen where his beautiful wife prepares dinner. In his hands he carries the very same toilet plunger, but this time not wrapped. He presents it to her and says, "Here sweetheart, I bought this for you."

Best-case scenario: She needed one and is pleased he picked it up, but looks at him with indifference and wishes it were flowers. Worst-case scenario: She looks at him like he is some sort of moron.

Finally, same man and woman: The woman walks into the bathroom to put away some towels. Next to the toilet she notices a brand new toilet plunger. She wanted one for a long time but kept forgetting to pick it up at the store. Apparently her husband took it upon himself to do it for her and put it where it belongs without mentioning it to her.

Worst-case scenario: She never says anything but is grateful. Best case: She comes out and asks, "Did you get the toilet plunger?" A simple shrug to the affirmative from her man and she gives him a hug thinking, "What a great guy I married."

The simple moral to this story is there are hundreds of gift ideas in this book that can be good gifts if the timing and presentation are correct. Stealth gifts are those making you look stupid if you wrap them up and give them to her as if they were something much more special. Go through the list, they are easy to spot. Stealth refers to the way in which you present her the gifts. The goal is to give them to her without actually giving them to her.

The nice thing about stealth gifts is their surprise nature. It means a lot to a woman when her man listens to her. If she complains about not having any tissues in the house and then one day finds them placed in all the right places, how happy will she be? What about dental floss, a new printer cartridge, hairspray, a dustpan, a pot-scrubber, a set of measuring spoons, a night light, a patio chair cover, and so on. Gifts do not have to be gift wrapped to be appreciated.

The thing differentiating stealth gifts from other gifts is in the style of praise you receive. You may or may not receive accolades for giving

> **List five items she needs and keeps forgetting to pick up.**
>
> _____
>
> _____
>
> _____
>
> _____
>
> _____

them. If she never finds them or does not put it together that you bought the items for her, she may never mention it to you. If she does know you gave them to her, she may get busy with life issues and never get around to thanking you. The accolades you receive may only come from the knowledge you did a very nice thing for your partner. More than likely however, she will notice and you will get your "thank you" in a timely fashion.

Regardless of whether you hear about it or not, she will appreciate the gesture and it will contribute to her overall attitude about you. How could she not appreciate a man who takes the time to listen to her needs, acts on what he hears, and does not look for acknowledgement for his deeds? Your value will climb in her eyes with every nonchalant gesture. Not a bad deal for you since you were already at the drugstore picking up a pack of gum when you saw that ninety-nine cent bottle of correction fluid for her desk just sitting there.

<u>Horror Story #117</u>

The Family Gathering

Sadly, yet another story emanates from my dear friend Debbie and her long time boyfriend. One Christmas season, after dating for many years, he came to her apartment and presented her with a small, wrapped jewelry-type box. Since she was traveling home for the holidays, she asked if she could open it immediately. He asked her to wait until her entire family surrounded her. He seemed very excited and she started getting a little nervous.

With the gift in tow, she went home to her family and informed them it was to be opened in their presence. Of course, you can imagine what all of them thought. Guesses emanated from every corner. Everyone had an opinion as to the contents. So, Christmas morning came and all the other gifts were opened. Debbie's ornately wrapped jewelry box was saved for the very last. With the entire family gathered around, Debbie slowly unwrapped the present. As the box creaked open, a wad of hair scrunches fell to the ground. Confused, Debbie and the family searched through them to discover what they might be concealing. Nothing was found.

So once again, Debbie called her boyfriend and asked about the gift. He excitedly told her, "You use those hair scrunches so often that I think of you every time I see them." Obviously he was the talk amongst the amazed and confused family for quite a while.

The simple moral to this story is two-fold. First, do not build up the importance of any gift if it truly doesn't deserve it. And second, never put any gift other than jewelry in a jewelry box.

Chapter 23

Theme Gifts

So you read the book, spent time on the Internet, visited your local bookstore, and you still have no clue what gift to give your sweetheart. You even went so far as to directly ask her what she wants. Of course, she gave you the same old line, "I have everything I want. I don't need anything special." After reading the chapter on the half-truths women tell, you know this is not the case. Stumped, you come to the realization you are in real trouble. Don't feel bad. We have all been there too. So what do you do next? Why not pick a theme? An entire gift-giving holiday can be based on a simple idea.

What are the top five activities she does for fun?

——————————

——————————

——————————

——————————

——————————

Ask yourself what she likes to eat, drink, and do for fun. This may give you the beginning of a tremendous gift-giving idea. What if she likes kayaking on the nearby lake? This can be a fantastic starting idea. Why not plan a vacation around that event? Plan a trip to the Pacific Northwest and stay at a secluded Bed & Breakfast. Early each morning you could sea kayak for hours through the Channel Islands off the coast of Washington. Maybe include an out of the way picnic, some disposable cameras for those extraordinary shots, and a flask filled with her favorite liquor. Too extravagant?

What if she loves camping but has not had the opportunity to go in quite some time? It is easy to fulfill this particular theme. You can wrap gifts including a lantern, sleeping bag, propane stove, and a map of the nearby wilderness area. Take some time off work so the minute she unwraps the gifts, you move her to the already packed car and head toward the mountains. Too spontaneous?

What if she likes wine? Make a date to go to the nearest winery or microbrewery. Often, they have classes to teach individuals how to bottle their own beverages. Give her the experience of making her own wine, designing her own labels, and taking cases home with her to drink on special occasions. Every time she opens a bottle of her own label, she will remember what you did for her. If this is too tame, take her to the California's Napa Valley or even France. Give her the opportunity to visit the wine country where many truly great wines originate. Not original enough?

If she likes driving her car fast, why not rent some time at a local speedway? Rent a really fast car for the day too. When you get there, have her open up a really nice set of driving gloves and some designer sunglasses. How fun would that be for both of you? When you get home, have a new racecar game for your kid's video game system already cued up.

The previous examples are only a few of thousands you can create for yourself. The only thing required of you is imagination. The smallest of ideas can be turned into something incredibly thoughtful and fun. If she likes breakfast in bed, why not take her to a hotel for a getaway and have room service bring your morning food?

If she likes working out, hire a professional trainer for a few sessions and give her some new workout gear. If she likes peaches, take her on a day trip to a local orchard and pick your own. On the way home, stop for and old-fashioned country dinner and some peach cobbler at an out of the way diner. It may sound silly, but truly great adventures start this way.

Even places she has already visited can be a source of great theme gift-giving potential. What is her favorite place of all time? Florence? Paris? How about Costa Rica, Hawaii, or New York? If she has not been to those destinations in some time and has no plans to return anytime soon, create a gift basket full of items to remind her of her special experience. Exotic foods, a miniature of the Eiffel Tower, a current newspaper or magazine from the city, postcards, magnets, mugs with images imbedded on them, tee shirts, and any other items which will nostalgically take her back to that time and location will be very much appreciated.

It does not matter what the theme is as long as it relates to her interests. A gift like this reeks of thought and caring. It shows you listen to her likes and dislikes and are doing what you can to make her feel special. That is what gifts should feel like in the first place.

Horror Story # 106

Thinking ahead, Valerie's boyfriend purchased some chocolates in a heart-shaped box a few days prior to Valentine's Day. To keep them fresh and away from her prying eyes, he hid them in the back of his freezer. Unfortunately, he didn't pull them out in time to thaw entirely. When Valerie took her first bite, she shattered one of her teeth.

Horror Story #132

Lisa's boyfriend went to Hawaii without her. On his way back from the airport, he realized he bought T-shirts, shell necklaces, magnets, and other novelty items for her two young daughters but he forgot to get Lisa anything. Thinking quickly, he took one of the novelty shell necklaces out of the girl's gift package and gave it to Lisa. She was not impressed.

Horror Story #138

Audrey was constantly complaining about the heat in her apartment. Apparently, it didn't have the proper circulation. For her twenty-fifth birthday, her boyfriend presented her with a tabletop fan and an indoor / outdoor thermometer.

Horror Story #151

Monica was upset with her body and spent hours in the gym working out. Standing in front of the mirror, she constantly pinched and poked at her areas of discontent. Her boyfriend, however, loved the way she looked and was mildly concerned about Monica's fixation. In the attempt to help her laugh at herself, he bought and installed a circus mirror in her bathroom. Let's just say that it didn't have the desired effect.

Chapter 24

Gift Baskets

I am a huge proponent of gift baskets. They are fun, easy to put together, and show lots of creativity. Similar to theme gifts, all you need to do is acquire a basket and fill it with items appropriate to any situation. If she loves bath time, fill a basket with all her favorite soaps, lotions, and fragrance products. Maybe include a big fluffy towel and some new bath slippers. How excited will she be to receive a gift like that one day?

What if she enjoys the opera? Try giving her a gift basket complete with Opera tickets, opera glasses, her favorite bottle of champagne, and two new champagne flutes.

If she enjoys horse racing, fill a basket with a daily racing form, the handicappers picks for the day, an envelope filled with two dollar bills for wagering, a new hat, new sunglasses, binoculars, and a flask filled with mint juleps.

Giving a gift basket can enhance any event or situation you can think of. Even in difficult times, a gift basket can brighten her day. For example, what if your wife has great difficulty dealing with a chauvinistic and abusive boss? She loves her job but despises the man. Most of the time, there is not much you can do but listen. One day, he has been especially nasty to her and she calls just to hear your loving voice. At this point, you have two choices: You can go down and beat the snot out of the jerk or you can find a way to be loving and supportive to her.

Choose the second. It may be less fulfilling in the short term but will not carry a jail term. Try having a gift basket delivered to her at work the next day. Inside, include: Ear plugs, a stress relieving squeeze ball, a miniature bottle of her favorite booze for when she really needs it, a toy gun that shoots suction cups instead of bullets, and a card from you saying, "I know you have had it rough lately and I just wanted you to know I love you."

Presenting her some humorous, tongue-and-cheek gifts will definitely not fix her problem but it might lighten the situation and will surely let her know you understand it. That can often go a long way toward helping her shed some of her stress.

Just like theme gifts, gift baskets relate solely to the individual you are giving them to. Any event in her life can be an opportunity for you to surprise her with a theme basket to celebrate or empathize with it. Have some fun here. With a little imagination and creativity you can brighten many of her days.

Chapter 25

Gift Preparation & Delivery

First, we are expected to give gifts to the women in our lives whether we like to receive them or not. Second, we spend gobs of time learning what she likes and dislikes. Third, we fight the crowds of people searching for the perfect gift in the attempt to make her happy for a least a short period of time. And now we have to package it and present it to her in some sort of exciting way? Does it never end?

> Giving gifts is very important because it shows we care. Creativity in the actual giving can show her how much we enjoy doing it.

Granted, there are many gifts needing no special buildup. Should you decide to give a woman a diamond necklace, there are very few ways to screw it up. I am quite sure most women would receive precious gems in almost any fashion and be quite grateful for them. That being said, you could make even a diamond necklace nicer if you wrap it in a beautiful package and give it to her during a romantic dinner.

The truth is that many men worry so much about getting just the right gift, they fail to consider the right way to present it. Again, if you are giving a toilet plunger or some correction fluid, I would suggest not making a big deal out of it. But if you are buying her an item to let her

know how special she is, take some time to make it feel
that way.

Paul and Debbie were giving their parents a ski trip for their
Anniversary. They rented a nice cabin and purchased airline tickets.
Instead of just handing their parents the tickets to this vacation getaway, Paul purchased toys from a thrift store consisting of miniature
chalets, houses, cabins, and trees. He also purchased some fake snow
and a set of miniature Christmas tree lights. He spent all of about
fifteen dollars. At home, he glued the buildings to a piece of cardboard
and backlit them with the miniature lights. After spreading the fake
snow all around, the miniature ski resort was complete. When their
parents came over, they saw the miniature ski village and were
completely surprised when presented with tickets and reservations.

In the above example, Paul spent about an hour
transforming an already wonderful gift into a giving
experience. You can do this with virtually any item you
buy.

The important thing to think about here is what will
make it fun for her. Would she be excited about you
coming through the door carrying a beautifully wrapped
gift or would she like to find a little something under her
pillow right before bed? Maybe she would be excited
about opening the refrigerator door before making supper
to find theatre tickets and dinner reservations for that
evening. The goal is to make a particular gift stand out
and become even more meaningful for her?

Creative gift giving yells loud and clear that we have
not only been thinking about her, but we have been
thinking about her for a long period of time. This can be
better than the actual gift could ever be. Take your time
and learn to enjoy the process. As you get more creative
with the way you give, you might start looking forward to
your next plan.

Chapter 26

Where To Search When Lost And Confused

Most men hate walking through malls hoping the perfect gift will jump out at them. There are those few men like my friend Paul who find inspiration perusing the stores, however those men are anomalies. Most men find moving from store to store, without any idea whatsoever, to be an exercise in futility. Remember, men shop differently than women. We know what we want, we go to the proper store, we get in, and more importantly we get out. That is the perfect shopping experience for a man. Therefore, ideas for gifts are golden. Especially if the ideas come before the shopping starts.

I have spent four hours walking aimlessly through every possible store in the mall and have purchased one refrigerator magnet, some cookies, and a four-in-one tool for myself. How much longer does this have to go on?

- Carl Hansen

Gift giving would not be such drudgery if men had some idea what the women in their lives wanted ahead of time. Life would be so much easier if gift ideas were easier to come by. So where can we go to get ideas?

First, and for no other reason than shameless self-promotion, this book is filled with thousands of potential gift ideas. The chapter entitled *Three Thousand Gift Ideas* alone has massive lists of potential gift items broken into specific categories. Go through them and check off the items she would like to own. Plus, if you truly take the time to fill out the questions about her likes, styles, and passions throughout this book, you will find many more gifts "jumping out at you" than ever before.

But, if for whatever reason you cannot find what you are looking for by leafing through the following pages, get your butt to a bookstore. Just stroll from aisle to aisle and you will likely discover hundreds of potential gift giving ideas. You may have to use some creative thinking, God forbid, but the ideas are there in abundance. In fact, you might even buy a book that interests her while you are searching. One gift out of the way.

What if you are lazier than that? No problem. Remember the chapter on E-gifts? Sit in front of your computer and check out the Internet. Go to your Internet browser and under the search category type in "gifts." Don't be surprised if you get more websites than you could look at in ten years. If you do not have a computer, your local library will. It also has books you can browse through. You can kill two birds with one stone.

Another place to get ideas is in her home. Utilize the time while she is in the shower, on the telephone, or shops at the grocery store to sit in the middle of each room and look around. What does she have? More importantly, what is she missing? This gift idea hunt does not take much time and carries the added attraction of sitting around on your backside doing virtually nothing.

> **The more you know about her, the easier the gift ideas will come to you.**

Her girlfriends can be a great resource as well. Even when you do not know what her likes and dislikes are, her friends will. They spend hours talking in depth about every aspect of each other's lives. Odds are they know more about her than you do. They will have lots of ideas and will likely be happy to share them if you feel the need to ask.

Finally you can apply for catalogs to be delivered to your home or office. This is a vast resource, as they put hundreds of potential gift ideas in one place. Like the previous gift idea search, you can order without having to get off your backside. And buying gifts through catalogs, as with the Internet, means the purchases will be delivered to you. You do not have to venture out to acquire the gifts yourself. At the very least, the catalogs will give you an enormous list of helpful ideas for when you actually do travel to the stores.

<u>WARNING!</u>

The substantial downside to catalog ordering is you get on those pesky mailing lists. Once on them, you might get catalogs from people and places you have never heard of for a very long time.

Once inside the stores, ask a sales clerk (female of course) for assistance. Don't be shy – that is why she's there. Ask about the items women are buying right now. Ask about the most popular fragrances, designer handbags, clothing trends, lingerie, and accessories. Ask about the newest and hottest designers, jewelry, and gadgets. The sales clerk will likely be able to answer all your questions and steer you in directions you hadn't thought of.

Ultimately, in your quest to find good gift giving ideas, you have the most valuable source of information already available to you. It is your significant other. She knows what she wants even when you do not. If you are stumped, ask her. Remember, she wants good gifts and will be more than happy to point you in a few good directions.

Chapter 27

Clothing & Fashion Accessories

Men have shirts, pants, socks, underwear, and shoes. Buying clothing for us is easy. We buy upscale clothing for dating and work, and we buy casual clothing for virtually everything else. Occasionally, we will buy specialty clothing for events, sporting needs, or to fit a particular trend, but overall our clothing is fairly predictable. There are quite a few designer men's clothing stores, but very few in relation to the sheer vastness of women's clothing designers and retail stores.

The Truth of It!

A little more than half the women interviewed thought men should avoid trying to buy them clothing. Nearly all the women agreed men are clueless when it comes to clothing styles and trends.

There are several issues to consider when shopping for women's clothing. First, women have forty-seven different names for everything. There are Ballet-neck dresses with soutache detail, mohair-blend slip dresses with lining, square neck knit dresses, linen camp shirts, trapeze dresses, jersey pants, capri pants, mock tops, and relaxed cotton sweaters. The only thing not relaxed will be you. Next, what styles does she like? There are cuffed, no cuff, draped, Victorian, western, renaissance, cropped, sequined, drawstring, fringe, beaded, ruffled and on and on and on.   Oddly, most women not only understand this language, they speak it fluently.   Men do not.   It is as if women were programmed from birth to speak this specialized lingo and told not to let the boys in on it.

When you want to buy her clothing, just say, "Honey, I want to buy you a new outfit," and take her shopping with you.
                                                    - Tanya Muncey

Rookie gift givers have no business venturing into this perilous world alone.   Clothing is as individual as the woman wearing it.   There are thousands of choices, if not hundreds of thousands, for each clothing item.   The manufacturers are pumping out different patterns and styles as quick as they possibly can.   Not only that, trends determined by the fashion world at this moment will fall out of style in a few months.   What other industry in the world advises you to buy their merchandise then months later tells you it is no good anymore and you should buy something else?

Clothing rules:
1.   Pay attention to what she wears and when she wears it
2.   Learn her sizes
3.   Find out about her favorite stores
4.   Go through her closets (with her permission, of course) to see what she already owns.
5.   Leaf through women's fashion magazines for ideas
6.   Until you know what you are doing: Take Her With You!

Clothes shopping is a skill you must develop over time.   You really have no choice.   More than half the stores in large shopping malls are clothing stores.   If you never learn how to buy clothing for her, you simply limit your gift choices even further.   But as is typical, many women don't make this easy for you.

When discussing this chapter with my friend Wynne, she scoffed at me and announced she would never tell me her dress size. I told her I didn't need to know it but someday her husband might. Her answer was, "Absolutely not!" After a moment of reflection she chuckled, "But then again, I'm not a size two. If I were a size two, I would wear it around my neck! I would wear a big neon sign: Check it out... I'm a size two. I'm a waif." She continued, "And who is a freaking size two anyway? I mean for God's sake, eat a cookie!" The laughter made it hard for me to catch my breath. Moments later, she added, "And what is a size zero? Those people need to be hospitalized." After this oration, I realized there are some women who just prefer to buy their own clothing.

Note to Women

Help your man. More than likely he has no clue about the clothing you like. Work with him but do it gently. Remember, he is a man. He is not preprogrammed for shopping prowess.

The first thing to consider when shopping for clothing is style. If your wife wears upscale clothing from trendy Italian designers, she may have a problem receiving a black leather jacket with silver spikes on the sleeves and chains draping from the sides. If she is a tomboy and wears only jeans and sweatshirts, what use do you think she will get out of a designer full-length ball gown? What if she dresses like a girl from the country? She might not have any use for a sequined disco-ball shirt and a pair of fluorescent plastic elevated shoes. Take some time figuring out just what her style is and you will successfully start the long journey toward suitable clothing gifts.

Clothing Styles

- ☐ Formal
- ☐ Vintage
- ☐ Western
- ☐ Victorian
- ☐ Casual
- ☐ Intimate
- ☐ Seasonal
- ☐ Southwestern
- ☐ Native American
- ☐ Fur
- ☐ Italian
- ☐ French
- ☐ Designer Fashions
- ☐ South American
- ☐ Asian / Oriental
- ☐ European
- ☐ Prairie
- ☐ Hip Hop
- ☐ Dyed
- ☐ Retro
- ☐ Gothic
- ☐ Adult
- ☐ Dominatrix
- ☐ Trendy
- ☐ Chic
- ☐ Athletic
- ☐ Medieval
- ☐ Indian
- ☐ Middle Eastern
- ☐ Mexican
- ☐ African
- ☐ Renaissance
- ☐ Business / Professional
- ☐ Safari
- ☐ Edwardian
- ☐ Military
- ☐ Punk
- ☐ Country
- ☐ Conservative
- ☐ Classic
- ☐ Sporty
- ☐ Beachy
- ☐ Tropical

Next, you have to determine what details she likes. Does she have a preference with regard to the animal pattern on her clothing or does she avoid loud patterns in all her choices? It should not take long to learn what clothing she currently wears. You can be sure the items she wears at this moment represent the style she prefers most.

Patterns

- ☐ Floral
- ☐ Pop Art
- ☐ Paisley
- ☐ Zebra Skin
- ☐ Leopard Skin
- ☐ Metallic
- ☐ Fringed
- ☐ Crocheted
- ☐ Macramé
- ☐ Embossed
- ☐ Beaded
- ☐ Studded
- ☐ Mesh
- ☐ Reversible
- ☐ Patchwork
- ☐ Braided
- ☐ Rhinestone
- ☐ Cheetah Skin
- ☐ Cow Skin
- ☐ Fossil
- ☐ Jeweled
- ☐ Neon
- ☐ Ocean Themed
- ☐ Sequined
- ☐ Striped
- ☐ Lace
- ☐ Ruffled
- ☐ Snakeskin
- ☐ Floral
- ☐ Angels
- ☐ Sunflower
- ☐ Seascape
- ☐ Checkerboard

☐ Wildlife	☐ Solid	☐ Pastel
☐ Mesh	☐ Logo	☐ Neon
☐ Lace	☐ Tropical	☐ Scalloped
☐ Pinstripe	☐ Festive	☐ Sheer
☐ Plaid	☐ Novelty	

Next, you must learn about fabrics. I realize it seems like the clothing lessons will never end, but you must nevertheless learn these items if you want to shop for women's clothing on your own. Each fabric and weave relates to a different thickness, style, and feel of the item you are buying. Can you imagine a pair of pajamas made out of Denim? Probably not the most comfortable night sleep she will ever have. Just remember the material making up the clothing is as important as size and style.

Note to Men

If confused about one fabric over another, ask a salesperson. They have an intimate knowledge of fashion and materials, and can be a great source of information for you.

Take some time talking with your sweetheart about the fabrics she likes most and what fabrics are best for different clothing items. Use the following as a guideline. You are not expected to know everything, but over time you should develop a working knowledge of her favorites.

Clothing Fabrics & Weaves

☐ Canvas	☐ Wool	☐ Snakeskin
☐ Cotton	☐ Angora	☐ Corduroy
☐ Denim	☐ Silk	☐ Linen
☐ Leather	☐ Polyester	☐ Gortex
☐ Velvet	☐ Suede	☐ Twill
☐ Satin	☐ Rayon	☐ Fleece

- ☐ Cashmere
- ☐ Fur
- ☐ Mink
- ☐ Chinchilla
- ☐ Fox
- ☐ Chiffon
- ☐ Crushed Velvet
- ☐ Faux Leather
- ☐ Taffeta
- ☐ Gingham
- ☐ Seersucker
- ☐ Terry Cloth
- ☐ Gabardine
- ☐ Cloth
- ☐ Nylon
- ☐ Spandex
- ☐ Challis
- ☐ Cheviot
- ☐ Donegal
- ☐ Felt
- ☐ Flannel
- ☐ Herringbone Wool
- ☐ Tweed
- ☐ Sharkskin
- ☐ Rabbit Hair
- ☐ Oatmeal Cloth
- ☐ Flannelette
- ☐ Gauze
- ☐ Muslin
- ☐ Oxford
- ☐ Velveteen
- ☐ Polished Cotton
- ☐ Sateen
- ☐ Sailcloth
- ☐ Charmeuse
- ☐ China Silk
- ☐ Faille
- ☐ Canton Crepe
- ☐ Matelasse
- ☐ Silk Broadcloth
- ☐ Silk Shantung
- ☐ Pongee
- ☐ Silk Satin
- ☐ Cardigan
- ☐ Angora
- ☐ Lycra

Gentlemen, the key to buying clothing is not to panic. Give yourself permission to make mistakes. You will make them. Even after forty years of marriage to my father, my mother often said, "This is great honey. Did you keep the receipt?"

Some women will not even consider clothing from a store that caters to bigger women. It is better to buy a XXL from a "thin store" than a normal size from a "fat store."

The following represent some of the thousands of clothing possibilities. Because of the vastness in styles, trends, materials, patterns, fashions and tastes, consider the following to be a very basic starting point for your skill development. Take some time going through the list with her. She will undoubtedly come up with ideas for you. Eventually, with patience and tenderness on her part, you will be able to shop for clothing without her help.

Blouses & Tops

- ☐ Camp Shirt
- ☐ Tunic
- ☐ Tee-Shirt
- ☐ Blouse
- ☐ Sweater
- ☐ Sweatshirt
- ☐ Caftan
- ☐ Crewneck Tee
- ☐ V-Neck Tee
- ☐ Pullover
- ☐ Peasant Top
- ☐ Tank Top
- ☐ Mock Top
- ☐ Vests
- ☐ Turtlenecks
- ☐ Logo Tops
- ☐ Novelty Tops
- ☐ Sport Shirts
- ☐ Work Blouses
- ☐ Trendy Tops

Dresses, Suits & Blazers

- ☐ Satin Gown
- ☐ Long Dress
- ☐ Evening Dress
- ☐ Crossback Dress
- ☐ Cocktail Dress
- ☐ Tank Dress
- ☐ Gingham Suit
- ☐ Slip Dress
- ☐ Ball Gown
- ☐ Belted Dress
- ☐ Skirt Suit
- ☐ Sleeveless Dress
- ☐ Halter Dress
- ☐ Strapless Dress
- ☐ Buckle Back Dress
- ☐ Strappy Dress
- ☐ Sundress
- ☐ Lace-up Gown
- ☐ Reversible Sundress
- ☐ Baby Doll Dress
- ☐ V-Neck Dress
- ☐ French Twist Dress
- ☐ Prairie Dress
- ☐ Jumpsuit
- ☐ Low Back Gown
- ☐ Peasant Dress
- ☐ Side Tie Dress
- ☐ Crinkle Lace Dress
- ☐ Open Back Blazer
- ☐ Lace Vest
- ☐ Crinkle Duster
- ☐ Business Suit
- ☐ Patchwork Dress
- ☐ Bolero Jacket

Jeans & Slacks

- ☐ Boot Cut
- ☐ Relaxed Fit
- ☐ Low Rider
- ☐ Tuxedo Jeans
- ☐ Multi-pocket Jeans
- ☐ Overalls
- ☐ Stretch Jeans
- ☐ Snap Front Jeans
- ☐ Cargo Pants
- ☐ Capri Pants
- ☐ Ski Pants
- ☐ Khakis
- ☐ Leather Pants
- ☐ Stretch Flare
- ☐ Pleat Front Jeans
- ☐ Straight Leg Jeans

- ☐ Elastic Sided Jeans
- ☐ Slit Leg Jeans
- ☐ Bleached Jeans
- ☐ Blast Finish Jeans
- ☐ Flat Front Pants
- ☐ Pantsuit
- ☐ Leggings
- ☐ Yoga Pants
- ☐ Western Cut
- ☐ Button Fly
- ☐ Bellbottom
- ☐ Carpenter Jeans

- ☐ Knit Pants
- ☐ Embroidered Capris
- ☐ Stretch Capris
- ☐ Parachute Pants
- ☐ Crepe Pants
- ☐ Army Surplus
- ☐ Drawstring
- ☐ Wide Leg
- ☐ Low Rise
- ☐ Maternity Pants
- ☐ Eyelet Pants
- ☐ Flood Pants
- ☐ Side Slit Pants

- ☐ Wide Waist Pants
- ☐ Hip Huggers
- ☐ Linen Pants
- ☐ Jazz Pants
- ☐ Gauchos
- ☐ Trousers
- ☐ Slacks
- ☐ Back Slit Pants
- ☐ Side Zip Pants
- ☐ Warm-up Pants
- ☐ Stirrup Pants
- ☐ Snap Pants

Shorts & Skirts

- ☐ Long Skirt
- ☐ Fishtail Skirt
- ☐ Stretch Skirts
- ☐ Bicycle Shorts
- ☐ Mini Skirts
- ☐ Dress Skirts
- ☐ Knee Length Skirts
- ☐ Ball Gown Skirt
- ☐ Carpenter Shorts

- ☐ Twill Shorts
- ☐ Prairie Skirt
- ☐ Wrap Skirt
- ☐ Long Shorts
- ☐ Utility Shorts
- ☐ Gym Shorts
- ☐ Pleated Skirt
- ☐ Drawstring Skirt
- ☐ Split Skirt
- ☐ Side Slit Skirts

- ☐ Boxer Shorts
- ☐ Cargo Shorts
- ☐ Athletic Shorts
- ☐ Jersey Skirts
- ☐ Button Front Skirts
- ☐ Petticoat Skirt
- ☐ Front Slit Skirt
- ☐ Denim Shorts
- ☐ Peasant Skirt

Footwear

- ☐ Athletic Shoes
- ☐ Sneakers
- ☐ Sandals
- ☐ Running Shoes
- ☐ Walking Shoes
- ☐ Cross Country Shoes
- ☐ Pumps

- ☐ Wedge Pumps
- ☐ Slides
- ☐ Mary Janes
- ☐ T-Strap Pumps
- ☐ Ankle Wraps
- ☐ Stretch Boots
- ☐ Snow Boots
- ☐ Sling-backs

- ☐ Mules
- ☐ Flats
- ☐ Wedges
- ☐ Skimmers
- ☐ Clogs
- ☐ Dressy Mules
- ☐ High Heel Sandals

- ☐ Lace-up Pumps
- ☐ Evening Pumps
- ☐ High Heel Pumps
- ☐ Thong Sandals
- ☐ Crisscross Sandals
- ☐ Loafers
- ☐ Buckled Sandals
- ☐ Buckled Pumps
- ☐ Hiking Boots
- ☐ Dress Boots
- ☐ Ankle Boots
- ☐ Knee High Boots
- ☐ Mid-calf Boots
- ☐ Side Zip Boots
- ☐ Riding Boots
- ☐ Stiletto Boots
- ☐ Shoe Boots
- ☐ Rain Boots
- ☐ Motorcycle Boots
- ☐ Casual Boots
- ☐ Granny Boots
- ☐ Demi Boots
- ☐ Slippers
- ☐ Moccasins
- ☐ Ballet Shoes
- ☐ Travel Slippers

> **Successful shoe buying is hard to do. If she wants shoes, needs shoes, or just loves shoes, take her with you to buy them.**

Lingerie & Sleepwear

- ☐ Camisole
- ☐ Bodysuit
- ☐ Bustier
- ☐ Tank Camisole
- ☐ Pajamas
- ☐ Babydoll w/ Thong
- ☐ Satin Gown
- ☐ Silk Robe
- ☐ Flannel Robe
- ☐ Waffle Robe
- ☐ Night Shirt
- ☐ Lounger
- ☐ Romper
- ☐ Long Robe
- ☐ Short Robe
- ☐ Kimono
- ☐ Flannel Pajamas
- ☐ Nightgown
- ☐ Slip Nightgown
- ☐ Lounge Pants
- ☐ Satin Pajamas
- ☐ Sleepshirt
- ☐ Silk Pullover
- ☐ G-String Panties
- ☐ Hi Cut Panties
- ☐ Thong
- ☐ String Thong
- ☐ Bikini Panties
- ☐ Tanga Panty
- ☐ Briefs
- ☐ Culotte Brief
- ☐ Boxers
- ☐ Shorties
- ☐ Hotpants Panty
- ☐ Low Brief
- ☐ Lace Panties
- ☐ Hipster
- ☐ French Cut Briefs
- ☐ Stretch Briefs
- ☐ String Bikini Briefs
- ☐ Tummy Shaper
- ☐ Skamp Briefs
- ☐ Slips
- ☐ Chemise
- ☐ Full Slip
- ☐ Half Slip
- ☐ Baby Doll
- ☐ Push Up Bra
- ☐ Corset Bra
- ☐ Full Figure Bra
- ☐ Sports Bra
- ☐ Nursing Bra
- ☐ Strapless Bra
- ☐ T-Shirt Bra
- ☐ Caftan
- ☐ Teddy
- ☐ Merrywidow
- ☐ Boyshorts

☐ Fun Panties
☐ Everyday Panties
☐ Sexy Panties

Socks

☐ Crew Socks
☐ Trouser Socks
☐ Knee Socks
☐ Hiker Socks
☐ Quarter Crew Socks

☐ Running Socks
☐ Tights
☐ Panty Hose
☐ Tube Socks
☐ Ski Socks
☐ Thermal Socks

☐ Low Cut Socks
☐ Bobbie Socks
☐ Shorties
☐ Snowboard Socks
☐ Footies
☐ Athletic Socks

Belts

☐ Equestrian Belt
☐ Harness Belt
☐ Hip Belt
☐ Beaded Belt
☐ G-buckle Belt
☐ Hipster Belt
☐ Ring Belt
☐ Link Belt
☐ Tapestry Belt
☐ Wide Belt
☐ Narrow Belt
☐ Tie Belt
☐ Fishnet Belt

☐ Reversible Belt
☐ Eye Belt
☐ Riveted Belt
☐ Studded Belt
☐ Double Grommet Belt
☐ Braided Belt
☐ Canvas Belt
☐ Mesh Belt
☐ Painted Belt
☐ Leather Belt
☐ Motorcycle Belt
☐ Hemp Belt

☐ Denim Belt
☐ Macrame Belt
☐ Web Belt
☐ Fringe Belt
☐ Woven Belt
☐ String Belt
☐ C-buckle Belt
☐ Embossed Belt
☐ Whipstitch Belt
☐ Rope Belt
☐ Novelty Belt

Hats

☐ Fedora
☐ Straw Hat
☐ Crusher Hat
☐ Engineer Hat
☐ Expedition Hat
☐ Beanie

☐ Walking Hat
☐ Hiking Hat
☐ Bicycle Hat
☐ Baseball Cap
☐ Bucket Hat
☐ Knit Cap

☐ Knit Cap with Pouf
☐ Gardening Hat
☐ Reversible Hat
☐ Novelty Hat
☐ Safari Hat

☐ Button Hat
☐ Pillbox Hat
☐ Sombrero
☐ Felt Hat
☐ Outback Hat

☐ Bell Hat
☐ Western Hat
☐ Rain Hat
☐ Passport Hat
☐ Hoods

☐ Headbands
☐ Fur Hat
☐ Visor

Purses & Handbags

☐ Demi Handbag
☐ Demi Pouch
☐ Messenger Bag
☐ Hobo
☐ Denim Handbag
☐ Oyster Bag
☐ Linen Handbag
☐ Square Handbag
☐ Small Tote
☐ Clutch
☐ Scallop Clutch
☐ Flap Bag
☐ Clamshell Bag

☐ Chain Clutch
☐ Medium Shopper
☐ Satin Bag
☐ Link Chain
  Envelope
☐ Large Clutch
☐ Small Clutch
☐ Baguette
☐ Wallet
☐ Logo Wallet
☐ Coin Purse
☐ Satchel
☐ Flat Pouch

☐ Key & Coin Pouch
☐ Pill Box
☐ Compact Clutch
☐ Business Card
  Case
☐ Travel Purse
☐ Scoop
☐ Wristlet
☐ Briefcase
☐ Backpack
☐ Logo Bag
☐ Novelty Bag
☐ Billfold

Miscellaneous Accessories

☐ Bikini
☐ One Piece
☐ Swim Skirt
☐ Swimdress
☐ Sarong
☐ Dress Gloves
☐ Casual Gloves
☐ Drawstring
  Mittens

☐ Mitts
☐ Ski Gloves
☐ Cashmere Gloves
☐ Leather Gloves
☐ Muffler
☐ Scarf
☐ Shawl
☐ Wrap
☐ Pashmina

☐ Sunglasses
☐ Cigarette Case
☐ Cell Phone Case
☐ Umbrella
☐ Eyeglass Case
☐ Key Fob
☐ Lipstick Case
☐ Business Card
  Holder

WARNING!

Do not even attempt to buy clothing after a pregnancy, even if you were good at it before. Avoid buying any items she will have to squeeze into. She will get depressed and angry. Imagine her reaction when you come home with a size twelve or XXL when she is accustomed to wearing size six. You might as well head for the door and get a beer. You cannot win in a post pregnancy situation with clothing. Don't even try. After pregnancy, your best bet is to buy her a diamond and tell her how lucky you are to have her in your life.

Chapter 28

Three Thousand Gift Ideas

This chapter is the one I dreamed about for years. As with most men, shopping is not my idea of a good time. It is a necessary evil. Every so often, when I need clothing or an appliance, I am left with no alternative but to run to the store and quickly pick it up doing as little damage to my free time as possible.

Most women, on the other hand, have a tremendous and peculiar love of shopping. It is their way to get out of the house and spend some much needed quality time on themselves. I know hundreds of women who can spend an entire day shopping and come back with two or three small items. Exhausted but exhilarated, they show off their new items and happily go about their business.

Not only do most men not understand this behavior, they would hate doing it. This is true even when buying gifts for their adoring spouses. They have no patience to sift through the hundreds of stores hoping just the right gift jumps out at them. Men prefer to know what they want in advance and head to the one store where it can be found with a minimum of difficulty. Shopping for men is a one-stop journey. Anything more becomes tedious and painful. They will even pay more for an item rather than waste time traveling to different stores to comparison shop.

> Somehow, the shopping gene was left out of man's DNA. If you see a man window-shopping, odds are he is actually trying to buy a window.

Well fellas... here it is. This chapter is dedicated to those of you who want to buy great gifts for your significant other but feel the pain of not knowing what to get. This chapter is filled with thousands of gifts and you only need to read through them and check off the ones sounding like a good idea. With this list, shopping should be so much easier than it ever has been before. If something sounds close to what she might like, check it off anyway. You may find a variation of the gift or personalize it to match her specifically. If you are still unsure, have her look through the list and check off the things you haven't thought of. Once you decide what to get her, you only need to find its location and make your one or two stops. The only problem now is deciding which gifts to get now and which ones can wait for another time.

Note To Men

As you wade through the following gifts, you should find hundreds of ideas to suit your sweetheart. But use a pencil. We all know she is likely to change her mind.

Antiques & Artwork

Art is a very subjective item. In my youth, I visited a museum in New York City and viewed many of the famous paintings on display. One of them was nothing but blue. No shades or highlights, just blue. It was confusing how such a seemingly bland painting could be so valuable and appreciated. In my opinion, it seemed as if a child could have painted it. Now I am no art critic and I never professed to be. I offer this story only because I would rarely be capable of purchasing a piece of art or sculpture for someone without checking with him or her first.

Just realize buying artwork for your significant other is not a matter of figuring out what you like, rather it is getting to know her style. Spending time with her, and around her stuff, is the only way to develop this skill. After a while, you will begin to see what she likes and picking out artwork might be a realistic and thoughtful gesture.

☐ Paintings
☐ Sculptures
☐ Tiles
☐ Autographed Pictures
☐ Caricatures
☐ Autographed Sports Paraphernalia
☐ Antique Musical Instruments
☐ Lithographs
☐ Sketches

☐ Celebrity Photographs
☐ Black & White Photography
☐ Pillars
☐ Fountains
☐ Vases
☐ Persian Rugs
☐ Antique Chess Set
☐ Carved Ivory
☐ Scales
☐ Tapestries

☐ Antique Telephone
☐ Foreign Carvings
☐ Hand Carved Bookends
☐ Antique Globe
☐ Antique Weaponry
☐ Antique Furniture
☐ Digital Art
☐ Gongs
☐ Masks

Automotive

Okay guys, we excel in this area. Well, most of us. My next book will likely be entitled, "Auto Maintenance and Repair for the Inept Man." Regardless, most women do not have the skill, patience, or desire to work on their cars. Also, why should money be spent on a car that could better be spent for a belt, a purse, some perfume, or an outfit? Now I realize there are many women out there who love their vehicles and who know far more about auto maintenance and repair than most men will ever know. For them, this category makes even more sense as potential gift giving ideas.

But a word of warning to those men who think working on their cars is a wonderful way to spend a day: Think long and hard before giving anything in this category to your sweetheart. You might find yourself sleeping in your car later that night.

- ☐ Floor Mats
- ☐ Seat Covers
- ☐ New Paint Job
- ☐ New Tires
- ☐ Car Alarm
- ☐ Radar Detector
- ☐ Tune-up
- ☐ Wiper Blades
- ☐ Oil Change
- ☐ New Stereo System
- ☐ Designer Car Parts
- ☐ Antenna Ball
- ☐ New Wheels
- ☐ Fuzzy Dice

- ☐ Auto Flashlight
- ☐ Emergency Road Service
- ☐ Car Air Freshener
- ☐ Waterproof Roof Carrier
- ☐ Trailer Hitch
- ☐ Towing Accessories
- ☐ Jumper Cables
- ☐ Remote Starters
- ☐ Dent Repair
- ☐ Road Atlas
- ☐ GPS System
- ☐ Cup Holders

- ☐ Auto Note Pad
- ☐ Window Sunscreen
- ☐ Visor Mirror
- ☐ Car Duster
- ☐ First Aid Kit
- ☐ Tire Gauge
- ☐ Thermal Coffee Mug
- ☐ Travel Inflatable Pillow
- ☐ CD Holder
- ☐ Emergency Flares
- ☐ Auto Tire Inflator
- ☐ Tinted Windows

Big & Expensive

Okay guys, this might be one category to skip over. If you don't have lots of expendable income, move on to the more intimate and romantic gifts. Not to suggest expensive gifts cannot be romantic, they are just pricey.

- ☐ New House
- ☐ Car
- ☐ Ski Boat
- ☐ Jet Ski
- ☐ Wave Runner
- ☐ Refrigerator
- ☐ Washer & Dryer
- ☐ Computer

- ☐ Laptop Computer
- ☐ Dishwasher
- ☐ Motorcycle
- ☐ Snowmobile
- ☐ Scooter
- ☐ All Terrain Vehicles
- ☐ Airplane

- ☐ Ultra-light Aircraft
- ☐ Hang Glider
- ☐ Scuba Equipment
- ☐ Ski Equipment
- ☐ Robot
- ☐ Tanning Bed
- ☐ Stove

- ☐ Mattress & Box Spring
- ☐ Swimming Pool
- ☐ Hot Tubs
- ☐ Piano
- ☐ Organ
- ☐ Misc. Musical Instruments
- ☐ Pool Table
- ☐ Precious Jewels
- ☐ Outdoor Jacuzzi
- ☐ Golf Equipment
- ☐ Home Theatre System
- ☐ Large Furniture Items
- ☐ Large Exercise Machine

Books & Magazines

Books can be a truly wonderful gift. If she likes to read, an interesting book can take her on a journey without her ever leaving the house. If she is crazy about a hobby or has interest in a particular subject matter, she will love any addition to her knowledge base. And books are great companions for travel and alone time. Buy them and buy them often. They are easy to acquire, usually inexpensive, and she will be grateful you thought of her.

The following is a list of book categories and topics. If you are not sure what she likes, spend some time perusing her bookshelves. The answer will be right in front of you.

- ☐ Fiction
- ☐ Non-fiction
- ☐ Cookbooks
- ☐ Women's Health
- ☐ Diseases
- ☐ Diet
- ☐ Exercise & Fitness
- ☐ Current Affairs
- ☐ Alternative Medicine
- ☐ Beauty & Grooming
- ☐ Wines & Spirits
- ☐ Medical Reference
- ☐ Nursing
- ☐ Psychotherapy
- ☐ Relationships
- ☐ Sexuality
- ☐ Self-improvement
- ☐ Psychology
- ☐ Addiction & Recovery
- ☐ Foreign Travel
- ☐ United States Travel
- ☐ Biography
- ☐ True Crime
- ☐ History
- ☐ Health
- ☐ Warfare
- ☐ Road Atlas's
- ☐ Reference
- ☐ Reading, Writing, & Publishing
- ☐ Gay & Lesbian
- ☐ Law
- ☐ Asian
- ☐ Legal Reference
- ☐ Cultural Studies
- ☐ Social Sciences

- ☐ Woman Studies
- ☐ Native American
- ☐ African-American
- ☐ Study Aids
- ☐ College Guides
- ☐ Large Print Books
- ☐ Wedding / Etiquette
- ☐ Language Books
- ☐ Management
- ☐ Success Library
- ☐ Personal Computing
- ☐ Computer
- ☐ Game Development
- ☐ Internet
- ☐ Graphics & Design
- ☐ Web Design
- ☐ Personal Finance
- ☐ Accounting
- ☐ Economics
- ☐ Investing
- ☐ Small Business
- ☐ Networking
- ☐ Marketing
- ☐ Advertising
- ☐ Careers
- ☐ Economy
- ☐ Science
- ☐ Business Motivation
- ☐ Dogs
- ☐ Cats
- ☐ Pets
- ☐ Nature
- ☐ Eastern Religion
- ☐ Judaica
- ☐ Religious Fiction
- ☐ Linguistics
- ☐ Philosophy
- ☐ Bibles
- ☐ Christianity
- ☐ Sports
- ☐ Spirituality
- ☐ New Age
- ☐ Astrology
- ☐ Religion
- ☐ Games
- ☐ Crafts
- ☐ Automobiles
- ☐ Gardening
- ☐ Home Reference
- ☐ Antiques & Collectibles
- ☐ Interior Design
- ☐ Humor
- ☐ Teens
- ☐ Technology
- ☐ Mathematics
- ☐ Romance
- ☐ Teaching Aids
- ☐ Education
- ☐ Children Books
- ☐ Science
- ☐ Fiction / Fantasy
- ☐ Graphic Novels
- ☐ Mystery
- ☐ Audio non-fiction
- ☐ Poetry
- ☐ Audio Self Help
- ☐ Audio
- ☐ Business
- ☐ Books on Tape
- ☐ Books on CD
- ☐ Mythology / Folklore
- ☐ Literary Theory
- ☐ Instrument / Instruction
- ☐ Music
- ☐ Rock & Roll
- ☐ Jazz / Blues
- ☐ Opera
- ☐ Film / TV / Radio
- ☐ Shakespeare
- ☐ Drama
- ☐ Theatre Arts
- ☐ Acting
- ☐ Fiction & Literature
- ☐ Photography
- ☐ Art
- ☐ Journals
- ☐ Architecture & Design
- ☐ Graphic Arts
- ☐ Art History
- ☐ Pregnancy & Childbirth
- ☐ Family & Childcare
- ☐ Inspirational Journals
- ☐ Sketch Books
- ☐ Address & Keepsake
- ☐ Picture Books
- ☐ Classics

Who are her favorite Authors?

_____   _____   _____

Magazines are a fantastic gift and there are thousands to choose from. Magazines are cool because you give her one subscription and a new gift comes every month. Each time your significant other sees her favorite magazine in the mailbox, she will likely think of you. A year's worth of giving in one swoop is not a bad way to go.

Listed below are many of the magazine categories. There are virtually hundreds of publications available in each. Check your local newsstand, library, and bookstore for publications she might be interested in. And don't forget the Internet. Surf through magazine WebPages, or for more ideas visit www.giftgivinghandbook.com.

☐ Animals	☐ Electronics	☐ Interior Design
☐ Antiques	☐ Entertainment	☐ Internet
☐ Art	☐ Environmental	☐ Lifestyle
☐ Audio	☐ Fashion	☐ Marketing
☐ Automotive	☐ Finance	☐ Medical
☐ Aviation	☐ Fishing	☐ Men's Issues
☐ Beauty	☐ Food / Cuisine	☐ Motorcycle
☐ Boating	☐ Games	☐ Music
☐ Business	☐ Gardening	☐ Mystery
☐ Children	☐ Golf	☐ Nature
☐ Collectibles	☐ Graphic Arts	☐ News
☐ Comics	☐ Health & Fitness	☐ Parenting
☐ Computers	☐ History	☐ Pets
☐ Cooking	☐ Hobbies	☐ Photography
☐ Crafts	☐ Home	☐ Political
☐ Cultural	☐ Home Repair	☐ Real Estate
☐ Cycling	☐ Horses	☐ Recreation
☐ Education	☐ Hunting	☐ Religion

- [ ] Sales
- [ ] Science Fiction
- [ ] Science
- [ ] Sports

- [ ] Tabloids
- [ ] Teen
- [ ] Television
- [ ] Travel

- [ ] Video
- [ ] Wines & Spirits
- [ ] Women's Issues

Candy & Sweets

Candy shopping for your wife is usually quite easy and will usually be appreciated by her. And in most cases, you can sample the merchandise while shopping. Consider it your reward for doing such a wonderful thing for her. Go through the following and check off her favorite flavors and favorite styles of confection.

What are her favorite Flavors?

- [ ] Milk Chocolate
- [ ] White Chocolate
- [ ] Dark Chocolate
- [ ] Caramel
- [ ] Toffee
- [ ] Red Raspberry
- [ ] Black Raspberry
- [ ] Peach
- [ ] Pear
- [ ] Cherry
- [ ] Lemon

- [ ] Lime
- [ ] Watermelon
- [ ] Apple
- [ ] Strawberry
- [ ] Blueberry
- [ ] Orange
- [ ] Tangerine
- [ ] Coconut
- [ ] Banana
- [ ] Pineapple
- [ ] Mango
- [ ] Apricot
- [ ] Dates
- [ ] Figs

- [ ] Maple Nut
- [ ] Peppermint
- [ ] Spearmint
- [ ] Cinnamon
- [ ] Pecan
- [ ] Walnut
- [ ] Almond
- [ ] Macadamia Nut
- [ ] Peanut
- [ ] Hazelnut
- [ ] Cashew

What are her favorite Candies?

- [ ] Saltwater Taffy
- [ ] Candy Bars
- [ ] Old Fashioned Candy
- [ ] Hard Candy

- [ ] Chewy Candy
- [ ] Gummy Candy
- [ ] Foreign Candy
- [ ] Black Licorice
- [ ] Red Licorice

- [ ] Peppermint Sticks
- [ ] Peanut Brittle
- [ ] Aplets
- [ ] Cotlets

- [ ] Bubble Gum
- [ ] Chewing Gum
- [ ] Jelly Beans
- [ ] Lollipops/Suckers
- [ ] Popcorn Tins
- [ ] Caramel Corn
- [ ] Sour Candy
- [ ] Candy Corn
- [ ] Pecan Chews
- [ ] Holiday Candy

- [ ] Liquor Filled Chocolates
- [ ] Malted Milk Balls
- [ ] Chocolate Covered Cherries
- [ ] Chocolate Covered Peanuts

- [ ] Chocolate Covered Raisins
- [ ] Chocolate Covered Pretzels
- [ ] Chocolate Covered Anything
- [ ] Other _____

What are her favorite Desserts?

- [ ] Shortbread Cookies
- [ ] Oatmeal Cookies
- [ ] Chocolate Chip Cookies
- [ ] Chocolate Cookies
- [ ] Macadamia Nut Cookies
- [ ] Coconut Cookies
- [ ] Gingerbread Cookies
- [ ] Brownies
- [ ] Fudge
- [ ] Sugar Cookies
- [ ] Tarts
- [ ] Banana Bread
- [ ] Mexican Wedding Cakes
- [ ] Date Nut Balls
- [ ] Holiday Cookies

- [ ] Macaroons
- [ ] Graham Crackers
- [ ] Devil's Food
- [ ] Donuts
- [ ] Crème Brule
- [ ] Custard
- [ ] Chocolate Mousse
- [ ] Soufflé
- [ ] Fruit Pies
- [ ] Cream Pies
- [ ] Pecan Pie
- [ ] Crumb Cake
- [ ] Blueberry Buckle
- [ ] Apple Crisp
- [ ] Strawberry Shortcake
- [ ] Fruit Cobblers
- [ ] Cheesecakes
- [ ] Angel Food Cakes
- [ ] Carrot Cake

- [ ] Pound Cake
- [ ] Rum Cake
- [ ] Sour Cream Cake
- [ ] Bundt Cake
- [ ] Red Velvet Cake
- [ ] Sponge Cake
- [ ] Coffee Cake
- [ ] Teramisu
- [ ] Petit Fours
- [ ] Baklava
- [ ] Sticky Buns
- [ ] Truffles
- [ ] Marzipan
- [ ] Ice Cream
- [ ] Sorbet
- [ ] Cherries Jubilee
- [ ] Baked Alaska
- [ ] Bon Bons
- [ ] Other_____

Cash & Gift Certificates

I only include this category because gift certificates can be a viable gift idea once you exhaust every other possibility. However, some consider cash and gift certificates to be the lazy man's way out. You should only purchase them at the very last minute after finding yourself out of ideas and still having people to buy for. There is, however, another school of thought.

After eighteen years of marriage and he has given everything he could possibly think of and it still isn't right, gift certificates are a great idea.

- Helaine Lembeck

Gift certificates are not romantic gifts. Wives and girlfriends may enjoy shopping and they may be thrilled with having the money available to them, but they will not look at you with admiration about your creativity. Give them if you want, and in all fairness you might find a perfect time to do it, however you might be selling yourself short. If you want her to be truly delighted, stick to romantic gifts she can unwrap.

Classes

If her biggest wish is more quality time with you, why not take a class together. This gift not only teaches a fun and potentially rewarding new skill, but it lets her know you enjoy her company as much as she enjoys yours. If you are too busy or she wants some alone time away from the family, classes can be a great break for her. Also, if she has a particular hobby or interest she actively pursues, continuing education classes are usually very appreciated. Her participation in the craft already lets you know how much she enjoys it. Classes to expand her knowledge base can be very rewarding for her.

Professional classes are available at most nearby community colleges as well as adult schools and individualized instruction on location or in your own home. Check your local yellow pages, the Internet, and perhaps a nearby bookstore for information.

- ☐ Computer Class
- ☐ Internet
- ☐ Jewelry Making
- ☐ Stained Glass
- ☐ Decoupage
- ☐ Mosaics
- ☐ Gift Basket Design
- ☐ Calligraphy
- ☐ Quilting
- ☐ Painting
- ☐ Singing
- ☐ Musical Instrument
- ☐ Flying School
- ☐ Floral Arranging
- ☐ Cooking
- ☐ Spiritual
- ☐ Adult & Child CPR
- ☐ Black Jack Class
- ☐ Furniture Refurbishing
- ☐ Meditation
- ☐ Yoga

- ☐ Photography
- ☐ Self Defense
- ☐ Conversationalist Training
- ☐ Feng Shui
- ☐ Golf
- ☐ Any Sport
- ☐ Massage
- ☐ Foreign Language
- ☐ Creative Writing
- ☐ Gemology
- ☐ Continuing Education Classes
- ☐ Candy Making
- ☐ Art & Sculpture
- ☐ Film Making
- ☐ Gardening
- ☐ Quilting
- ☐ Wood Working
- ☐ Needlework
- ☐ Crochet
- ☐ Macramet
- ☐ Embroidery
- ☐ Weaving
- ☐ Sewing

- ☐ Egg Decorating
- ☐ Model Building
- ☐ Mosaics
- ☐ Candle Making
- ☐ Beading
- ☐ Jewelry Making
- ☐ Ornament Making
- ☐ Kaleidoscope Artistry
- ☐ Origami
- ☐ Tattooing
- ☐ Clown School
- ☐ Latin Dancing
- ☐ Hip Hop Dancing
- ☐ Country Dancing
- ☐ Hula Dancing
- ☐ Ballroom Dancing
- ☐ Belly Dancing
- ☐ Cultural Dance
- ☐ Misc. Dance
- ☐ Other

_____

Cleaning Supplies

Don't do it! Don't even think about it! No matter what you believe you can get away with, you cannot pull this off. And besides, how much fun would it be for her to open a dustpan, a bottle of floor wax, and a pot scrubber for Christmas? Unless it is some type of humorous inside joke, you will likely find yourself on the business end of the broom you just gave her.

Collectibles

It is very easy to acquire new gift giving ideas for individual collections. Filling the gaps is the name of the game. Take a look to see if she has a particular collection then find an important item or two she does not yet own. If she doesn't have a collection started, maybe the following will give you some ideas about starting one for her.

- ☐ Sport Cards
- ☐ Sports Memorabilia
- ☐ Stamps
- ☐ Ivory Animals
- ☐ Train Sets
- ☐ Piggy Banks
- ☐ Christmas Ornaments
- ☐ Angels
- ☐ Dolls
- ☐ Doll Houses
- ☐ Teddy Bears
- ☐ Animals
- ☐ Handbags
- ☐ Coins
- ☐ Antique Beaded Purses
- ☐ Autographs
- ☐ Political Memorabilia
- ☐ Country Store Products
- ☐ Corkscrews
- ☐ Wristwatches
- ☐ Soda Pop Memorabilia
- ☐ Plates

- ☐ Jewelry
- ☐ Toys
- ☐ Beer Memorabilia
- ☐ Buttons
- ☐ Comic Books
- ☐ Figurines
- ☐ Books
- ☐ Photographs
- ☐ Postcards
- ☐ Records
- ☐ Depression Glass
- ☐ Pottery
- ☐ Snow Globes
- ☐ Bells
- ☐ Golf Memorabilia
- ☐ Bottle Stoppers
- ☐ Glassware
- ☐ Bottles
- ☐ Spoons
- ☐ Mugs
- ☐ Hats
- ☐ Magazines
- ☐ Cookie Tins
- ☐ Celebrity Memorabilia
- ☐ Comic Books
- ☐ Movie Memorabilia

- ☐ Thimbles
- ☐ Lunchboxes
- ☐ Greeting Cards
- ☐ Automotive Memorabilia
- ☐ Shells
- ☐ Trading Cards
- ☐ Miniatures
- ☐ Paper Dolls
- ☐ Music Boxes
- ☐ Antique Games
- ☐ Gumball Machines
- ☐ Costume Jewelry
- ☐ Ivory Carvings
- ☐ Miniature Iron Stoves
- ☐ Wartime Paraphernalia
- ☐ Antique Marbles
- ☐ Vases
- ☐ Renderings
- ☐ Cherubs
- ☐ Perfume Bottles
- ☐ Teapots
- ☐ Teacups
- ☐ Merry-go-round Animals

Before adding to a collection, learn as much as you can about it. Avoid buying cheap imitations of collection pieces or items not quite representing the collection. She will feel obligated to display them.

Cooking & Kitchen

Remember the previous chapters and the warnings contained in their pages. Birthdays, Valentine's Day, wedding anniversaries, and any other romantic days are not a time to buy cooking related items for your special someone. Consider yourself warned.

However, cooking and kitchen items are great gifts for the professional chef, the amateur chef, or anyone who really enjoys entertaining. These items can also make good filler gifts at Christmas and other holidays. There are many reasons and numerous occasions to give her stuff for the kitchen, but again you should pick and choose your spots very carefully.

☐ Cookware
☐ Coffee Maker
☐ Coffee Grinder
☐ Cappuccino Machine
☐ Tea Kettle
☐ Toaster Oven
☐ Knife Set
☐ Knife Sharpener
☐ Food Processor
☐ Waffle Maker
☐ Vegetable Slicer
☐ Vacuum Sealer
☐ Pressure Cooker

☐ Crock pot
☐ Sauce Pan
☐ Frying Pan
☐ Colander
☐ Mixing Bowls
☐ Utensil Set
☐ Slotted Spoon
☐ Balloon Whisk
☐ Locking Tongs
☐ Ladle
☐ Measuring Cups
☐ Flat Whisk
☐ Skimmer
☐ Fish Turner

☐ Tomato Slicer
☐ Blender
☐ Egg Cooker
☐ Buffet Warming Tray
☐ Ice Cream Maker
☐ Wok
☐ Stove
☐ Gourmet Slicer
☐ Scale
☐ Smoothie Maker
☐ Bundt Pan
☐ Ice Shaver
☐ Cooking Torch

- Pastry Board Set
- Paring Knives
- Pepper Mills
- Chopping Mats
- Kitchen Shears
- Bread Knife
- Poultry Shears
- Cleaver
- Boning Knife
- Spinning Salad Mixer
- Roasting Pan
- Espresso Maker
- Grill Press
- Deep Fryer
- Sponge
- Sponge Caddy
- Wine Cooler
- Dish Drainer
- Food Grinder
- Plates
- Bowls
- Cups
- Flatware
- Hand Mixer
- Toaster
- Pizzelle Maker
- Skillet
- Panini Grill
- Dessert Plates
- Steamer
- Bar Starter Set
- Cups & Saucers
- Ice Cube Trays
- Covered Stockpot
- Casserole Pan
- Roasting Pan
- Square Griddle
- Egg Ring
- Copper Canister Set
- Can Opener
- Electric Can Opener
- Percolator
- Tupperware
- Egg Platter
- Peelers
- Olive Oil Mister
- Cutting Board
- Oven Mitts
- Spatula Set
- Kitchen Island Cart
- Tomato Holder
- Nutcracker
- Cheese Slicer
- Garlic Roaster
- Prep Bowls
- Crepe Maker
- Cake Pan
- Jelly Roll Pan
- Cookie Sheet
- Muffin Pan
- Grease Keeper
- Avocado Slicer
- Scoops
- Frozen Popsicle Mold
- Carafe
- Meat Pounder
- Cheese Grater
- Apple Slicer / Corer
- Lasagna Pan
- Kitchen Towels
- Bread Maker
- Trash Can
- Smoker Cooker
- Food Dehydrator
- Canister Set
- Gravy Boat
- Cookie Press
- Thermometer
- Double Broiler
- Beverage Dispenser
- Plate Warmer
- Condiment Cups
- Herb Mincer
- Timer Clock
- Salsa Server
- Flatbread Maker
- Butcher Block
- Corkscrew
- Napkins
- Ice Crusher
- Cocktail Shaker
- Coasters
- Martini Set
- Spices
- Spice Rack
- Fondue pan
- Drawer Organizer
- Margarita Glasses
- Snifters
- Decanter
- Cookie Jar
- Wine Opener
- Oven Mitt
- Hot Plate
- Vegetable Steamer
- Ramekins
- Cookbooks
- Wooden Bowls
- Pitchers
- Butter Dish
- Napkin Rings
- Storage Containers
- Dish Clothes

- ☐ Pasta Maker
- ☐ Juicer
- ☐ Tea Strainer
- ☐ Spice Ball
- ☐ Pancake Molds
- ☐ Wine Rack
- ☐ Refrigerator Magnet
- ☐ Coffee Mugs
- ☐ Dishwasher
- ☐ Refrigerator
- ☐ Garbage Disposal

- ☐ Melon Baller
- ☐ Pasta Holder
- ☐ Paper Towel Dispenser
- ☐ Magnetic Knife Rack
- ☐ Plastic Bag Dispenser
- ☐ Microwave Oven
- ☐ Martini Glasses
- ☐ Shot Glasses
- ☐ Rocks Glasses

- ☐ Highball Glasses
- ☐ Champagne Flutes
- ☐ Wine Glasses
- ☐ Popcorn Popper
- ☐ Strainers
- ☐ Serving Platters
- ☐ Flatware
- ☐ Hot Plate
- ☐ Novelty Apron

Electronics

Many women love gadgets and electronic things too. It is not just the men. However, this can be one of the most rewarding shopping experiences you encounter. Why? Think of how many items you will locate for yourself while shopping for her. Have fun. You deserve it.

- ☐ Desktop Computer
- ☐ Radio
- ☐ Travel Clock
- ☐ Alarm Clock
- ☐ VCR
- ☐ Clock Radio
- ☐ Tape Recorder
- ☐ DVD Player
- ☐ Telephone
- ☐ Cordless Telephone
- ☐ Desktop Computer
- ☐ Laptop Computer
- ☐ Printer

- ☐ Scanner
- ☐ Fax Machine
- ☐ Camcorder
- ☐ Digital Camera
- ☐ Television
- ☐ TV/VCR Combo
- ☐ Universal Remote Control
- ☐ Stereo
- ☐ Speakers
- ☐ Home Theatre System
- ☐ CD Player
- ☐ Portable CD Player
- ☐ Telescope

- ☐ Karaoke Machine
- ☐ Microphone
- ☐ Headphones
- ☐ Boom Box
- ☐ Electronic Keyboard
- ☐ Pinball Machine
- ☐ PDA
- ☐ Global Positioning System
- ☐ Travel Reading Light
- ☐ 35mm Camera
- ☐ Disposable Camera

- [ ] Instant Camera
- [ ] Digital Camcorder
- [ ] Mini Tape Recorder
- [ ] Key Chain Flashlight
- [ ] Solar Powered Lights
- [ ] Satellite Dish
- [ ] Two-way Radio
- [ ] Baby Monitor
- [ ] Micro Camera (Nanny Monitor)
- [ ] Pedometer
- [ ] Air Purifier
- [ ] Ultrasonic Pest Repellent

- [ ] Shower CD Player
- [ ] Shower Radio
- [ ] Cellular Telephone
- [ ] Microwave Oven
- [ ] Blender
- [ ] Electric Blanket
- [ ] Copier
- [ ] Scale
- [ ] Vacuum Cleaner
- [ ] Space Heater
- [ ] Magnifiers
- [ ] Metal Detectors
- [ ] Radar Detectors
- [ ] Weather Gauges
- [ ] Telescope
- [ ] Lighting

- [ ] Space Heater
- [ ] Vacuum Cleaner
- [ ] Portable Vacuum Cleaner
- [ ] Sewing Machine
- [ ] Steam Cleaner
- [ ] Washing Machine
- [ ] Dryer
- [ ] Air Conditioner
- [ ] Insect Control Devices
- [ ] Remote Controlled Vehicles
- [ ] Remote Controlled Aircraft

Experiences

The great thing about experiences is you can design an entire holiday of gift giving around one idea. As mentioned previously, new experiences make people feel alive. Try one of these and see how excited she gets. Do not just rely solely on this list either. It is virtually impossible to list every conceivable new experience. Just listen to what she says and come up with new experience ideas on your own. And remember, many things you have previously experienced and find mundane might be new and exciting to her.

- [ ] Hot Air Ballooning
- [ ] Helicopter Ride
- [ ] Drive to a New State
- [ ] Snowmobiling

- [ ] White Water Rafting
- [ ] Rollerblading
- [ ] Skateboarding
- [ ] Roller-skating
- [ ] Jet Skiing

- [ ] Mountain Biking
- [ ] Scuba Diving
- [ ] Surfing
- [ ] Ice Skating
- [ ] Throw a Costume Party

- ☐ Throw a Goofy Shoe Party
- ☐ Throw any kind of Theme Party
- ☐ Plant a Tree
- ☐ Fishing
- ☐ Go to Museums & Cultural Centers
- ☐ Teach her to Drive
- ☐ Fly an Aircraft
- ☐ Pottery Class
- ☐ Bottle Your Own Wine / Beer
- ☐ Visit a Zoo
- ☐ Take her to a Fireworks Show
- ☐ Go to a Professional Sporting Event
- ☐ Experience Snow
- ☐ Hunting
- ☐ A Train Ride
- ☐ Spelunking
- ☐ Swimming with Dolphins
- ☐ Hang-gliding
- ☐ Skydiving
- ☐ Whale Watching
- ☐ Surprise Party
- ☐ Swimming with Sharks
- ☐ Karaoke
- ☐ Go on a Picnic
- ☐ Sailing
- ☐ Take her to an Aquarium
- ☐ Snorkeling
- ☐ Canoeing
- ☐ Tropical vacation
- ☐ Attend a Concert
- ☐ Row Boating
- ☐ Build a Ginger Bread House
- ☐ Plant a Vegetable Garden
- ☐ Puppet Show
- ☐ Treasure Hunt
- ☐ Horseback Riding
- ☐ Camping
- ☐ Cooking Class
- ☐ Fondue Party
- ☐ Skateboarding
- ☐ Snow Skiing
- ☐ Tobogganing
- ☐ Take her to a Water Park
- ☐ Cross Country Skiing
- ☐ Visit a Dairy Farm
- ☐ Pick Blueberries
- ☐ Visit a Winery
- ☐ Steam Bath at an Indian Sweat Lodge
- ☐ Go on a Cruise
- ☐ Visit the Ocean
- ☐ Visit the Desert
- ☐ Stargazing
- ☐ Make your own Chocolates
- ☐ Visit Foreign Lands
- ☐ Magic Show
- ☐ Las Vegas Style Show
- ☐ Attend the Theatre
- ☐ Live Taping of her Favorite Television Show
- ☐ Visit a Volcano
- ☐ Sit in Natural Hot Springs
- ☐ Bungee Jumping
- ☐ Visit a Ghost Town
- ☐ Nature Hike in the Mountains
- ☐ Repelling
- ☐ Mountain Climbing
- ☐ Visit a Ruby Mine
- ☐ Dig for Gold
- ☐ Spend Night in a Haunted House
- ☐ Go on Safari
- ☐ Rent a Beach House
- ☐ Visit the Pope
- ☐ Make Sushi Together
- ☐ Big City Dining
- ☐ Go to a Race Track
- ☐ Saltwater Fishing
- ☐ Shooting a Gun
- ☐ Martial Arts
- ☐ Watch a Shuttle Takeoff
- ☐ Storm Hunting
- ☐ Make a Pilgrimage to Religious Site
- ☐ An Air Show
- ☐ Dune Buggy Ride
- ☐ Go to National Convention
- ☐ Candle Making
- ☐ Get a Bee Farm
- ☐ Go Crabbing
- ☐ Fly a Kite

- ☐ Go to a Race Track
- ☐ Visit Hollywood
- ☐ Go to a Theme Park
- ☐ Visit the Pyramids
- ☐ Visit Wonders of the World
- ☐ Rent a Houseboat
- ☐ Beachcombing
- ☐ Learn to Swim
- ☐ Volunteer
- ☐ Sheer a Sheep
- ☐ Milk a Cow
- ☐ Take a River Cruise
- ☐ Dinner Cruise
- ☐ Alaskan Cruise
- ☐ Parasailing
- ☐ Windsurfing
- ☐ Metal Detecting
- ☐ Bull Riding
- ☐ Go to Drive-in Movie
- ☐ Go to a Rodeo
- ☐ Gamble at a Casino
- ☐ Visit Fisherman's Wharf
- ☐ Sea Kayaking
- ☐ Bird Watching
- ☐ Travel on Submarine
- ☐ Eat Exotic Foods
- ☐ Visit the Everglades
- ☐ Cattle Rustling
- ☐ Treasure Hunt
- ☐ Tickets to the Olympics
- ☐ Appointment with Psychic
- ☐ Palm Reading
- ☐ Visit Historical Places
- ☐ Champagne Brunch
- ☐ Rent a Limousine

Flowers

There are hundreds of flowers and flowering plants to choose from. There are equally as many colors and bright patterns in the blooms. Take every opportunity you can to experiment with new vases and bouquets. Chances are if you like it, she will too. If you lack confidence in your floral arranging skills, have the florist suggest something. In fact, if you describe the situation to her, the florist might create something unique and exciting right there on the spot. You don't need to have a working knowledge of floral arranging to give flowers as a gift.

What are her favorite Flowers?

- ☐ Lily
- ☐ Snap Dragon
- ☐ Daisy
- ☐ Marigold
- ☐ Lilacs
- ☐ Cherry Blossoms
- ☐ Orange Blossoms
- ☐ Orchids
- ☐ Carnations
- ☐ Dogwood Blooms
- ☐ Poinsettias
- ☐ Gardenias
- ☐ Gladiolus
- ☐ Sunflowers
- ☐ Hibiscus

☐ Hydrangeas   ☐ Geraniums   ☐ Pansy
☐ Iris   ☐ Roses   ☐ Mistletoe
☐ Lavender   ☐ Rhododendron   ☐ Impatiens
☐ Honeysuckle   ☐ Willow   ☐ Petunias
☐ Daffodil   ☐ Goldenrods   ☐ Zinnias
☐ Lotis   ☐ Tulips   ☐ Wildflowers
☐ Oleander   ☐ Violets   ☐ Peonies

The only thing to remember is to buy flowers and buy them as often as possible. It is a delightful way to show her you love her.

Food: Gourmet, Traditional, Etc.

Unique snacks and specialty foods are a great gift, especially if your spouse loves to eat. And, there are endless new items out there waiting to be discovered. There are traditional and gourmet food items not venturing too far from her normal menu and extreme, adventurous items she has never dreamed of. Why not take a risk and add some new tastes into her world?

Even if she is not much of a risk taker, a bag of gourmet chocolate brownies from a trendy coffee shop is not too much of a stretch. And look at it this way, if she does not enjoy them, she will still feel good you took the time to think of her. And best of all, you are entitled to eat the rest of them. Nice, huh?

There is not a problem in the world a doughnut can't fix.
- **Pat Schnabel**

What if she is a risk taker with regard to food? What if she likes Indian foods, Middle Eastern foods, and other ethnic tastes? Create some fun for her by going into specialty shops and coming home with a few new delicacies for her to sample.

Whatever her taste preferences, the following list contains food items made in many different ways. There are many gourmet, designer, and international food outlets carrying a myriad of products to try. If your town lacks in variety, get online to find wonderful new food experiences. You can also visit my website at www.giftgivinghandbook.com for more ideas. I have links to several gourmet and international food companies. Have fun and enjoy the good eats.

☐ Salsas
☐ Dips
☐ Mustards
☐ Chutneys
☐ Salad Dressings
☐ Olive Oils
☐ Spreads
☐ Butters
☐ Honeys
☐ Pestos
☐ Breads
☐ Crackers
☐ Croissants
☐ Cheeses
☐ Pastas
☐ Soups
☐ Spices
☐ Herbs
☐ Meats
☐ Seafood
☐ Caviar
☐ Relishes
☐ Tapenades
☐ Truffles

☐ Designer Teas
☐ Designer Coffee
☐ Cookies
☐ French Pastries
☐ Bakery Goods
☐ Designer Candies
☐ Fruit Baskets
☐ Jellies & Jams
☐ Sugar Free Foods
☐ Snack Foods
☐ Holiday Foods
☐ Dried Fruits
☐ Dried Meats
☐ Dried Vegetables
☐ Seasonal Fruits
☐ Regional Foods
☐ International Foods
☐ Sushi Making Supplies
☐ Marinades
☐ Rubs
☐ Syrups
☐ Salts

☐ Vinegars
☐ Hot Sauces
☐ Glazes
☐ Nuts
☐ Vegetables
☐ Grains
☐ Baking Mixes
☐ Smoked Foods
☐ Drink Mixes
☐ Alcoholic Beverages
☐ Non-Alcoholic Beverages
☐ Canned Foods
☐ Survival Foods
☐ Frostings
☐ Puddings
☐ Custards
☐ Pies
☐ Cakes
☐ Desserts
☐ Dessert Toppings
☐ Ice Creams

Gadgets

Gadgets refer to novelty items that make her life easier, more productive, or more entertaining. Gadgets can be useful, whimsical, or just clutter collecting dust. Regardless, they are usually fun to get even if they never get used. Now that being said, more men feel the passion for quirky little items than women. Gadgets are things guys just love to collect. So, slow down. The impulse to buy lots of these items, because they are clever and readily available, will be very strong.

All you need to do before purchasing a gadget is ask yourself, "Will she truly appreciate this item or do I love it so much that I think everyone else will too?" The answer to that question will dictate whether you should buy her one or not.

- Air Injecting Wine Opener
- Shoe Stretchers
- Can Dispenser for Refrigerator
- Massaging Chair
- Telephone Headset
- Micro Tool Kit
- Voice Changer
- Parking Distance Sensor
- Digital Compass
- Travel Pillow
- Book Light
- Digital Picture Frame
- Key Chain Flash Light
- Microwaveable Ice Cream Scoop
- Miniature Camera
- Battery Conversion Kit
- Color Coded Keys
- Beverage Warmer
- Snow Cone Maker
- Massaging Jet Spa
- Personal Cooling System
- A Safe
- Coin Sorter
- Electric Tweezers System
- Ultrasonic Bug & Rodent Repeller
- Underwater Camera
- Guillotine Cigar Cutter
- Wrist Blood Pressure Monitor
- Blowup Mattress
- Simulated Video Security Camera
- Telescoping Duster
- Telescoping Light Bulb Changer
- Lifetime Light Bulb
- Rain Shower Showerhead
- Electronic Tooth Brush
- Bicycle Pedestal
- Robot Vacuum
- Ear Warmers
- High Pressure Sprayer
- Insect Vacuum

☐ Soothing Sound Machine
☐ Telephone Conversation Recorder
☐ Reading Pen
☐ Translation Pen
☐ Suction Cup Mirror
☐ Compression Socks
☐ Underwater Pen
☐ Solar Powered Lights
☐ Submersible Bag
☐ Space Pen
☐ Button Machine
☐ Hot Lather Machine
☐ Heated Lotion Dispenser
☐ Door Wedge
☐ Magnifying Glass
☐ Waistband Stretcher
☐ Tap Lights
☐ Indoor Watering Hose
☐ Photo Key Chain
☐ Car Vacuum

☐ Night Vision Goggles
☐ Money Clip
☐ Laser Pointer
☐ Upside-Down Writing Pen
☐ Six Egg Cooker
☐ Waterproof Telephone
☐ Mini-Refrigerator
☐ Wave Machine
☐ Shower Radio
☐ Ultrasonic Toothbrush
☐ Automatic Bill Counter
☐ Heated Lounging Pillow
☐ Bottle Dispenser
☐ Cordless Vacuum
☐ Motion Detector
☐ Shower Multi-Chamber Soap Dispenser
☐ Shower Seat
☐ Telescoping Bike Rack
☐ Remote Controlled CD Player

☐ Digital Breath Alcohol Tester
☐ No Battery Needed Flashlight
☐ Water Resistant Portable Television
☐ Miniature Wine Cellar
☐ Cordless Air Compressor
☐ Telescoping Ladder
☐ Wireless Doorbell
☐ Magnifying Mirror
☐ Reaching Tool
☐ Lint Shaver
☐ Telephone Amplifier
☐ Automatic Card Shuffler
☐ Smoothie Machine
☐ Inverted Bottle Liquor Dispenser
☐ Bubble Gum Machine

Games

If quality time is important to your spouse, a night at home playing games might be just what she needs to feel loved. Maybe she likes entertaining friends with countless dinner parties and weekend get-togethers. A new party game might make the night even more festive.

There are plenty of toys and games to choose from. Just visit your local toy store or get online to locate a new game or one of the many old favorites.

Indoor Games

☐ Party Games
☐ Get Together Games
☐ Adult Themed Board Games
☐ Drinking Board Games
☐ Card Games

☐ Trivia Games
☐ Family Games
☐ Strategy Games
☐ Arcade Games
☐ Billiards
☐ Backgammon
☐ Chess
☐ Darts

☐ Foosball
☐ Table Tennis
☐ Video Games
☐ Computer Games
☐ Tile Games
☐ Puzzles
☐ Crossword Puzzles

Outdoor Games

☐ Volleyball
☐ Badminton
☐ Croquet
☐ Horseshoes

☐ Archery
☐ Bocce
☐ Beach Games
☐ Paddle Ball

☐ Games for the Swimming Pool
☐ Shuffleboard

Health & Beauty

Take a look at the differences in products designed for men and women. Men have "soap." Harsh and tough, soap is designed to get the oil, grime, and general gunk off their rough callused hands and fingernails. Women, on the other hand, have moisturizers, spritzers, sprays, and creams. They have gels, scrubs, salts, and lotions. They have oils, balms, mists, splashes, essences, serums, acids, washes, soufflés, and body butters. Again, men have soap. Why do women have all these products? Partly for cleanliness but more often than not women use these products for beauty and feel.

The following list contains items to help your special someone feel pampered and pretty. Put together a gift basket with everything she might need to improve her bathing experience. Bath accessories can be a very romantic gift if presented in the right way.

WARNING!

Some items in this category may be taken the wrong way. Do not buy an electric nose hair trimmer and expect her to be thrilled. Imagine her look of surprise when she unwraps it and comes to the conclusion you think she has too much hair in her nose. Read the chapter on stealth gifts if you intend to purchase items such as these.

□ Massages
□ Facials
□ Pedicures
□ Manicures
□ Facial Scrubs
□ Soaps
□ Bath Beads
□ Bath Gels
□ Soft Body Buffers
□ Bathing Glove
□ Designer Soap
□ Lip gloss
□ Scented Bath Oils
□ Floating Candles
□ Foot Soak & Scrub Kit
□ Body Butter
□ Nose Hair Trimmer
□ Travel Hygiene Kit
□ Loofahs
□ Massage Oils
□ Massage Lotion

□ Scrub Mitt
□ Sponge
□ Vitamins
□ Back Scrubber
□ Lip Balms
□ Face Mists
□ Foot Spray
□ Leg Gels
□ Mineral Foot Bath
□ Foot Files
□ Bath Foam
□ Foot Massagers
□ Neck Massager
□ Aroma Therapy Candles
□ Hand Lotion
□ Hand Cream
□ Makeup Bag
□ Bath Travel Bag
□ Bubble Bath
□ Hand & Nail Treatments
□ Salt Scrub

□ Sleep Mask
□ Body Splash
□ Shower Gel
□ Aroma Therapy Bath Salts
□ Body Creams
□ Sugar Scrubs
□ Pillow Mists
□ Bath Pillow
□ Bath Robe
□ Bath Slippers
□ Liquid Gel Mask
□ Moisturizing Gel Sleeves
□ Spa Sandals
□ Moisture Socks
□ Foot Creams
□ Soothing Makeup Remover
□ Nourishing Eye Cream
□ Facial Scrubs
□ Sensual Body Essence

- ☐ Therapeutic Body Wrap
- ☐ Massaging Chair
- ☐ Copper Belt
- ☐ Body Buffer
- ☐ Incense Burner
- ☐ Incense
- ☐ Shower Radio
- ☐ Electric Shaver
- ☐ Hair Brush
- ☐ Tooth Brush
- ☐ Powders
- ☐ Creams & Lotions
- ☐ Serums
- ☐ Sprays
- ☐ Masks
- ☐ Gels
- ☐ Complexes

- ☐ Acids
- ☐ Washes
- ☐ Body Soufflés
- ☐ Oils
- ☐ Mud Masks
- ☐ Moisture Gloves
- ☐ Body Powders
- ☐ Exfoliaters
- ☐ Pulsating Toothbrush
- ☐ Shiatsu Massagers
- ☐ Vitamin Skin Care
- ☐ Waxing kit
- ☐ Various Skin Care Systems
- ☐ Steam Inhaler

- ☐ Digital Thermometer
- ☐ Professional Makeover
- ☐ Massaging Bubble Mat
- ☐ Calming Sound Machine
- ☐ Scalp Massager
- ☐ Comfy Towels
- ☐ Jacuzzi
- ☐ Pulsating Shower Head
- ☐ Tinted Contact Lenses
- ☐ Magnetic Brace
- ☐ Facial Steamer

Cosmetics may be very foreign to us, but we do like our women to look beautiful. It works perfectly because they like to feel beautiful too. The following represents a list of cosmetic items she more than likely possesses already. But take note of what she has and keep your ears open for opportunities.

Note to Men

Women are very faithful to their own cosmetic brands and colors. Do not try to surprise her with new cosmetic products. Just learn what she likes and replace them if necessary.

- ☐ Blush
- ☐ Concealer
- ☐ Eye Shadow
- ☐ Eye Liner
- ☐ Eye Enhancer
- ☐ Eye Shadow Base

- ☐ Heated Eye Lash Curler
- ☐ Lash Primer
- ☐ Brow Liner
- ☐ Brow Styling Gel
- ☐ Foundation

- ☐ Glitter
- ☐ Nail Care System
- ☐ Nail Polish
- ☐ Nail Polish Remover
- ☐ Nail Clippers

- ☐ Nail Treatments
- ☐ Nail Enamel
- ☐ Nail Nylon
- ☐ Nail Teflon
- ☐ Nail Repair Kit
- ☐ Nail Base Coat
- ☐ Nail Top Coat
- ☐ Nail Grower
- ☐ Nail Conditioner
- ☐ Nail Strengthener
- ☐ Cuticle Care
- ☐ Cuticle Oil
- ☐ Acrylic Nails
- ☐ Designer Nails
- ☐ Lipstick
- ☐ Lip Gloss
- ☐ Lip Liner
- ☐ Lip Sealer
- ☐ Lip Polish

- ☐ Lip Moisturizer
- ☐ Pencils
- ☐ Powders
- ☐ Pigments
- ☐ Paints
- ☐ Mascara
- ☐ Cordless Shaver
- ☐ Brushes
- ☐ Hand Held Massagers
- ☐ Cosmetic Applicators
- ☐ Makeup Remover
- ☐ Whip Liner
- ☐ Tweezers
- ☐ Cuticle Scissors
- ☐ Jaw Nippers
- ☐ Half Jaw Nippers
- ☐ Nail Buffer

- ☐ Nail Clipper
- ☐ Toenail Clipper
- ☐ Emery Boards
- ☐ Pumice Stone
- ☐ Barrel Spring Nipper
- ☐ Accent Brush
- ☐ Contour Brush
- ☐ Face Brush
- ☐ Lip Brush
- ☐ Applicators
- ☐ Sponges
- ☐ Blotters
- ☐ Travel Brushes
- ☐ Pencil Sharpener
- ☐ False Eyelashes
- ☐ Toe Spacer
- ☐ Make-up Cases

There are few things more frustrating to women who love their hair than to run out of products they need. Keep your eyes and ears open. You may find an opportunity to come to the rescue.

- ☐ Hair Dryer
- ☐ Brushes
- ☐ Curling Iron
- ☐ Clips
- ☐ Hair Claws
- ☐ Barrettes
- ☐ Wraps
- ☐ Banana Combs
- ☐ Hair Scrunchies
- ☐ Stretch Combs
- ☐ Salon Clips
- ☐ Head Bands

- ☐ Hair Sticks
- ☐ Designer Hair Pins
- ☐ Rollers
- ☐ Spider Clips
- ☐ Hair Removal Systems
- ☐ Hair Spray
- ☐ Hair Gel
- ☐ Spritzer
- ☐ Designer Shampoo

- ☐ Conditioner
- ☐ Styling Mouse
- ☐ Foam
- ☐ Professional Salon Appt.
- ☐ Bobby Pins
- ☐ Straightening Iron
- ☐ Hair Masks
- ☐ Head Bands

Home Accessories

Like buying clothing, when choosing items for her home you must first take into account her personal style and tastes. If you give a fluorescent plastic dining room table and chairs, a zebra patterned love seat, and an acrylic nude statue to a woman who likes a warm country environment, you failed miserably.

Spend a little time looking at her possessions to discover her style preferences and what materials she would likely enjoy. Then, when you have made a decision regarding a particular furniture item, refer back to the following two lists to make sure which style will fit her décor.

Furniture Styles

☐ Victorian	☐ Fluorescent	☐ Unfinished
☐ Western	☐ Formal	☐ Ergonomic
☐ Mosaic	☐ Comfortable	☐ Designer
☐ Vintage	☐ Palatial	☐ Spanish
☐ Southwestern	☐ Country Home	☐ Mexican
☐ Native American	☐ Hi-tech	☐ Retro
☐ Antique	☐ Casual	☐ Country
☐ Contemporary	☐ Hand Carved	☐ Roman
☐ Futuristic	☐ Rustic	☐ Rustic
☐ Italian	☐ Reproduction	☐ Modern
☐ South American	☐ Art & Artifact	☐ Shabby Chic
☐ European	☐ Inflatable	☐ Early American
☐ Asian / Oriental	☐ Mission	☐ Children's
☐ Egyptian	☐ Outdoor	
☐ Middle Eastern	☐ African	

Furnishing Materials

☐ Brass	☐ Rattan	☐ Cloth
☐ Glass	☐ Wicker	☐ Porcelain
☐ Acrylic	☐ Rope	☐ Depression Glass
☐ Hardwood	☐ Bird's Eye Maple	☐ Feather
☐ Bamboo	☐ Cherry	☐ Copper
☐ Oak	☐ Walnut	☐ Stainless Steel
☐ Pine	☐ Stainless Steel	☐ Plastic
☐ Velvet	☐ Pressboard	☐ Chrome
☐ Leather	☐ Plastic	☐ Marble
☐ Suede	☐ Fur	☐ Stained Glass
☐ Denim	☐ Down	☐ Damask
☐ Canvas	☐ Mahogany	☐ Granite
☐ Crystal	☐ Redwood	☐ Tapestry
☐ Snakeskin	☐ Wrought Iron	
☐ Hemp	☐ Cedar	

Now take some time going through the following list to discover some potentially wonderful home additions. You will likely find several items to make her environment more functional and cozy.

☐ Wine Rack	☐ Wardrobe Valet	☐ Newspaper Rack
☐ Mirror	☐ Sofa	☐ Wine Glass Rack
☐ Wall Sconces	☐ Piano	☐ Shelving for
☐ Candle Holders	☐ Chair	Garage
☐ Rugs	☐ Recliner	☐ Shoe Caddie
☐ Welcome Mat	☐ Armoire	☐ Flag Pole
☐ New Curtains	☐ Oriental Rug	☐ Step Stool
☐ Iron and Ironing	☐ Floor lamp	☐ Ottoman
Board	☐ Magazine Rack	☐ Wall Lamp
☐ Flash Light	☐ Vanity mirror	☐ Hanging Lamp
☐ Space Heater	☐ Shower caddy	☐ Electric Fan
☐ Telescoping	☐ Mattress & Box	☐ Ceiling Fan
Duster	Spring	☐ CD Holder
☐ Key Rack	☐ Drawer Organizer	☐ Candelabra
☐ Hamper	☐ Cabinet Stackers	☐ Fountain

- ☐ Artwork
- ☐ Wind Chimes
- ☐ Stereo System
- ☐ Television
- ☐ Home Theatre System
- ☐ Bird Feeder
- ☐ Couch Pillows
- ☐ Wall Clocks
- ☐ Bedding
- ☐ Picture Frames
- ☐ Cord of Firewood
- ☐ Designer Chess Set
- ☐ Fireplace Bellow
- ☐ Fireplace Screen
- ☐ Coasters
- ☐ New Cabinets
- ☐ New Cabinet Knobs
- ☐ Tapestries
- ☐ Bookends
- ☐ Globe
- ☐ Drop Leaf Table
- ☐ Plant Stand
- ☐ Silk Flowers
- ☐ Mantle Clock
- ☐ Tea Caddy
- ☐ Wall Telephone
- ☐ Cordless Telephone
- ☐ Candle Sconce
- ☐ Humidifier
- ☐ Dehumidifier
- ☐ Desk Fan
- ☐ Floor Screen
- ☐ Air Purifier
- ☐ Water Purifier
- ☐ Floor Fan
- ☐ Umbrella Stand
- ☐ Coat Rack

- ☐ Coffee Table
- ☐ End Tables
- ☐ Sofa Table
- ☐ Antique Chests
- ☐ Corner Cupboard
- ☐ Weather Vane
- ☐ Towel Rack
- ☐ Air Mattress
- ☐ Comforter Set
- ☐ Sheet Set
- ☐ Pillows
- ☐ Electric Blanket
- ☐ Wall Mirror
- ☐ Console Table
- ☐ Mattress Pad
- ☐ Entertainment Center
- ☐ Window Blinds
- ☐ Dining Set
- ☐ Grandfather Clock
- ☐ Display Cabinet
- ☐ Bookcase
- ☐ Lounge Chair
- ☐ Barstools
- ☐ Tray Table
- ☐ Baskets
- ☐ New Carpet
- ☐ Cushions
- ☐ Wall Shelf
- ☐ Chest of Drawers
- ☐ Lamp Shade
- ☐ Potted Plant
- ☐ Sculpture
- ☐ Painting
- ☐ Candlesticks
- ☐ Speakers
- ☐ Speaker Mounts
- ☐ Track Lighting
- ☐ Speaker Stands
- ☐ Sheepskin Rug

- ☐ Reading Lamp
- ☐ Work Lamp
- ☐ Storage Unit
- ☐ Easy Chair
- ☐ Swivel Chair
- ☐ Bookcase

Lighting
- ☐ Throw
- ☐ Wardrobe Light
- ☐ Loveseat
- ☐ CD Storage Rack
- ☐ Room Divider
- ☐ Sofa Bed
- ☐ Chaise
- ☐ Television Bench
- ☐ Multimedia Rack
- ☐ Armchair
- ☐ Futon
- ☐ Standing Mirror
- ☐ Hard Wood Flooring
- ☐ Slipcovers
- ☐ Sofa Blanket
- ☐ Lounging Pillow
- ☐ Rocking Chair
- ☐ Corner Shelf
- ☐ Piano Bench
- ☐ Lighting Fixtures
- ☐ Tablecloths
- ☐ Centerpieces
- ☐ Tea Lights
- ☐ Bedside Tables
- ☐ Quilt
- ☐ Shower Curtain
- ☐ Trash Compactor
- ☐ Trash Can
- ☐ Soap Dish
- ☐ Shower Caddie
- ☐ Bath Mat
- ☐ Butcher Block Table

- ☐ Vases
- ☐ Sewing Cabinet
- ☐ Air Purifier
- ☐ Barstools
- ☐ Step Ladder
- ☐ Daybed
- ☐ Bench
- ☐ Persian Rug
- ☐ Shutters
- ☐ Oriental Rug
- ☐ Space Heater
- ☐ Recliner
- ☐ Suit of Armor
- ☐ Brass Wall Shelf
- ☐ Chandelier
- ☐ Magazine Tower
- ☐ Curtain Tassels

- ☐ Curtain Rods
- ☐ Curtains
- ☐ Ottoman
- ☐ Accent Table
- ☐ Foot Locker
- ☐ Fish Pot
- ☐ Accent Chair
- ☐ Duvet
- ☐ Lingerie Chest
- ☐ Ornate Vent Covers
- ☐ Musical Instruments
- ☐ Trundle Bed
- ☐ Blankets
- ☐ Quilts
- ☐ Photo Album

- ☐ Cuckoo Clock
- ☐ Floor Vases
- ☐ Table Centerpiece
- ☐ Dining Set
- ☐ Serving Table
- ☐ Decorative Bottles
- ☐ Decorative Bowls
- ☐ Folding Table
- ☐ Folding Chairs
- ☐ Step Stool
- ☐ Marble Pedestal
- ☐ Television Pedestal
- ☐ Bar Stool
- ☐ Display Cabinet

Jewelry

Jewelry is as individual as the person wearing it. Your wife may wear many pieces of jewelry every day or perhaps only on special occasions. She may prefer understated stones and settings or she may like big and gaudy. Leaf through her jewelry box, with her permission of course, to determine what style of jewelry she likes best. Watch what she wears on casual days out and when she dresses to impress.

Note to Men

Bracelets, rings, necklaces and every other jewelry item are available in virtually thousands of unique styles and materials. Although jewelry is easier to pick out than clothing, you still must develop an eye for what she likes.

Rings & Settings

- ☐ Solitaire
- ☐ Channel Set
- ☐ Pave Set
- ☐ Wrap Channel
- ☐ Cluster

- ☐ Claw Set
- ☐ Multi-Stone
- ☐ Eternity
- ☐ Sweep
- ☐ Bezel

- ☐ Filigree
- ☐ Pinky Ring
- ☐ Puzzle Ring
- ☐ Toe Rings

Necklaces

- ☐ Pave Set
- ☐ Pendant

- ☐ Chain
- ☐ Bezel Set

Chains

- ☐ Wheat
- ☐ Rope
- ☐ Cable
- ☐ Herringbone

- ☐ Curb
- ☐ Box
- ☐ Ball
- ☐ Figure Eight

- ☐ Snake
- ☐ Waist Chains
- ☐ Ankle Chains

Bracelets

- ☐ Tennis
  Bracelet
- ☐ Cross Link

- ☐ Ankle
  Bracelets

- ☐ Charm
  Bracelets

Earrings

- ☐ Cluster
- ☐ Hoop
- ☐ Stud
- ☐ Drop Hook

- ☐ Basket
- ☐ Dangle
- ☐ Flat Pad
- ☐ Loop

- ☐ Tube
- ☐ Screw Post
- ☐ Leverback
- ☐ Ear Clip

Watches

- ☐ Jeweled
- ☐ Dress

- ☐ Casual
- ☐ Sports

- ☐ Dive
- ☐ Novelty

Pendants & Brooches

☐ Basket   ☐ Fancy   ☐ Sterling Silver
☐ Wire   ☐ Coin Frame
☐ Multi-stone   ☐ Cast Wire

Body Piercing

☐ Tongue Jewelry   ☐ Navel Jewelry   ☐ Nipple Rings
☐ Eyebrow Jewelry   ☐ Nose Jewelry

Precious metals are a very important consideration. Women usually prefer one style of metal over all others. If the color silver is their preference, consider buying settings in white gold or platinum. Traditional yellow gold may be marvelous, but you want the jewelry to be something she will enjoy and wear often.

Which precious metal does she prefer?

☐ Gold   ☐ Platinum   ☐ Sterling Silver
☐ Silver   ☐ White Gold

Precious and semi-precious stones come in a myriad of colors. Although most women would love anything from the following list, many have preferences to color, size, and shape of the stones they wear. If you are not sure, start with her birthstone set in a nice bracelet or necklace. But don't be bashful about asking her. She will undoubtedly get much pleasure telling you about the jewelry she prefers and why. In fact, the anticipation of the impending gift of jewelry can be an added bonus for her.

Which are her favorite stones?

☐ Ruby
☐ Emerald
☐ Sapphire
☐ Diamond
☐ Pearl
☐ Opal
☐ Amethyst
☐ Aquamarine
☐ Topaz
☐ Turquoise
☐ Tanzanite
☐ Agate
☐ Alexandrite
☐ Amber
☐ Citrine
☐ Garnet
☐ Iolite
☐ Jade

☐ Lapis
☐ Malachite
☐ Moonstone
☐ Onyx
☐ Quartz
☐ Zircon
☐ Flourite
☐ Jasper
☐ Labradorite
☐ Morganite
☐ Tiger's Eye
☐ Sugilite
☐ Unakite
☐ Sunstone
☐ Tourmaline
☐ Cinnabar
☐ Cobalt Calcite
☐ Beryl

☐ Ametrine
☐ Idocrase
☐ Hematite
☐ Amazonite
☐ Aventurine
☐ Spinel
☐ Indicolite
☐ Cornelian
☐ Obsidian
☐ Peridot
☐ Sodalite
☐ Nephrite
☐ Chrysoberyl
☐ Serpentine
☐ Rubellite
☐ Misc. Crystals

The cut of a jewel can be as important to your sweetheart as any other feature. Many jewelry items do not need special attention regarding the cut, but do not skip this important detail for the really big jewelry gifts.

What is her favorite cut?

☐ Emerald Cut
☐ Pear Shaped
☐ Princess

☐ Heart Shaped
☐ Marquise
☐ Teardrop

☐ Oval
☐ Baguette
☐ Trillion

Birthstones

Birth Month	Traditional Birthstone	Zodiac Sign	Zodiac Birthstone
January	Garnet	Capricorn (Dec. 21- Jan. 20)	Ruby
February	Amethyst	Aquarius (Jan. 21 – Feb. 20)	Garnet
March	Aquamarine, Bloodstone	Pisces (Feb. 21 – Mar. 21)	Amethyst
April	Diamond	Aries (Mar. 22 – Apr. 19)	Bloodstone
May	Emerald	Taurus (Apr. 20 – May 20)	Sapphire
June	Pearl, Alexandrite, Moonstone	Gemini (May 21 – June 21)	Agate
July	Ruby	Cancer (June 22 – July 21)	Emerald
August	Sardonyx	Leo (July 22 – Aug. 20)	Onyx
September	Sapphire	Virgo (Aug. 21 – Sep. 20)	Cornelian
October	Tourmaline, Opal	Libra (Sep. 21 – Oct. 21)	Peridot
November	Citrine	Scorpio (Oct. 22 – Nov. 21)	Aquamarine
December	Zircon, Turquoise, Blue Topaz	Sagittarius (Nov. 22 – Dec. 20)	Topaz

Liquor

Booze comes in almost any flavor you can imagine. By now, you have surely spent enough time with your honey to know what she likes to drink. In fact, many of you probably met your significant other in a bar. Regardless, liquor can be a nice gift as well as a lubricant to get an entertaining evening started.

What are her favorite Beverages?

Beer
- [ ] Ambers
- [ ] Ales
- [ ] Pilsners
- [ ] Lagers
- [ ] Light Beer
- [ ] Dark Beer
- [ ] Domestic
- [ ] Microbrew
- [ ] Mexican
- [ ] Canadian
- [ ] Japanese
- [ ] Chinese
- [ ] Australian
- [ ] English
- [ ] German
- [ ] Dutch

White Wine
- [ ] Chardonnay
- [ ] Sauvignon Blanc
- [ ] Pinot Grigio
- [ ] Pouilly-Fuisse
- [ ] Fume Blanc
- [ ] Rhine
- [ ] Chablis
- [ ] Riesling

Red Wine
- [ ] Cabernet Sauvignon
- [ ] Merlot
- [ ] Chianti
- [ ] Bordeaux
- [ ] Beaujolais
- [ ] Pinot Noir
- [ ] Burgundy
- [ ] Zinfandel

Blush Wine
- [ ] White Zinfandel
- [ ] Rose

Champagne
- [ ] Extra Dry
- [ ] Brut
- [ ] Rose

Misc. Wine
- [ ] Sherry
- [ ] Cream Sherry
- [ ] Sangria
- [ ] Gewurztraminer
- [ ] Shiraz
- [ ] Port
- [ ] Sake

Liquor
- [ ] Vodka
- [ ] Flavored Vodkas
- [ ] Gin
- [ ] White Rum
- [ ] Dark Rum
- [ ] Flavored Rums
- [ ] Gold Tequila
- [ ] White Tequila
- [ ] Bourbon
- [ ] Scotch
- [ ] Brandy
- [ ] Cognac

Liqueurs
- [ ] Schnapps
- [ ] Triple Sec
- [ ] Cream Liqueurs
- [ ] Coffee Flavored
- [ ] Whisky Based
- [ ] Cinnamon
- [ ] Peppermint
- [ ] Spearmint
- [ ] Chocolate
- [ ] White Chocolate
- [ ] Hazelnut
- [ ] Almond

Misc. Liquor
☐ Aperitifs
☐ Dry Vermouth
☐ Sweet Vermouth
☐ Hard Ciders
☐ Hard Colas
☐ Hard Lemonades
☐ Premixed Drinks

Accessories

☐ Blender
☐ Ice Shaver
☐ Margarita Glasses
☐ Martini Glasses
☐ Wine Glasses
☐ Snifters
☐ Champagne Glasses
☐ Pilsner Glasses
☐ Beer Steins
☐ Cocktail Shakers
☐ Strainers
☐ Olives
☐ Olive Picks
☐ Cocktail Onions
☐ Maraschino Cherries
☐ Fruit Garnishes
☐ Drink Mixers
☐ Straws
☐ Drink Napkins
☐ Pitcher
☐ Glass Rim Salter
☐ Corkscrew
☐ Bottle Opener
☐ Liquor Canisters
☐ Serving Tray
☐ Decorative Cocktail Stirs
☐ Champagne Bucket
☐ Ice Tongs
☐ Bottle Stoppers
☐ Drink Guide

Movies

Make a list of her favorite movies of all time, then slowly build her collection of VHS tapes or DVD's. You might build a collection based on her favorite celebrity or favorite director. On those cold, quiet nights, she will be very grateful to have her favorite movie to curl up to.

What is her favorite Genre?

☐ Action / Adventure
☐ Adult
☐ Animation
☐ Art House
☐ Black Comedy
☐ Buddy Movies
☐ Chick Films
☐ Comedy
☐ Coming of Age
☐ Crime
☐ Cult Films
☐ Disaster
☐ Documentaries
☐ Drama
☐ Educational
☐ Epics
☐ Family
☐ Fantasy
☐ Film Noir
☐ Foreign Films
☐ Horror
☐ Independent
☐ Love Stories
☐ Musical
☐ Mystery
☐ Mythical

- ☐ Romantic Comedy
- ☐ Science Fiction
- ☐ Silent Films
- ☐ Social Drama
- ☐ Suspense
- ☐ Thriller
- ☐ War Movies
- ☐ Westerns

What are her top five favorite movies of all time?

_____ _____ _____

_____ _____

Who are her top five favorite celebrities?

_____ _____ _____

_____ _____

Music

Easy and good for any occasion, music is important to many people. Just go through her CD's and find what she listens to. Too many artists to list here but the genre of music is just as important. Write down her favorite artist and her favorite genre of music then go to your local music store and see if that artist has a new album out. She will love the addition to her collection.

- ☐ Aboriginal
- ☐ Accordion
- ☐ Acid Jazz
- ☐ Alternative
- ☐ Ambient
- ☐ Arabic
- ☐ Asian
- ☐ Avant-Garde
- ☐ Fifties
- ☐ Sixties
- ☐ Seventies
- ☐ Eighties
- ☐ Nineties
- ☐ Banjo
- ☐ Bass
- ☐ Big Band
- ☐ Blue Grass
- ☐ Blues
- ☐ Bubble Gum
- ☐ Cabaret
- ☐ Calypso
- ☐ Caribbean
- ☐ Cello
- ☐ Christian
- ☐ Christmas
- ☐ Clarinet
- ☐ Classic Jazz

☐ Classic R&B
☐ Comedic
☐ Country
☐ Country Rock
☐ Dance
☐ Disco
☐ Easy Listening
☐ Exercise
☐ Exotica
☐ Flamenco
☐ Flugelhorn
☐ Flute
☐ Folk
☐ Freestyle
☐ French Horn
☐ Funk
☐ Fusion
☐ Girl Groups
☐ Gospel
☐ Gothic
☐ Grunge
☐ Guitar
☐ Hard Rock
☐ Harmonica
☐ Harp

☐ Hip Hop
☐ Honkytonk
☐ House
☐ Instrumental
☐ International
☐ Jazz
☐ Jazz Vocal
☐ Karaoke
☐ Latin
☐ Mambo
☐ Mandolin
☐ March
☐ Mariachi
☐ Meringue
☐ Modern Jazz
☐ Motown
☐ Musicals
☐ New Age
☐ Oldies
☐ Organ
☐ Percussion
☐ Piano
☐ Polka
☐ Polynesian
☐ Pop

☐ Pop Metal
☐ Pop R & B
☐ Pop Vocal
☐ Progressive
☐ Psychedelic
☐ Punk Rock
☐ R&B
☐ Rap
☐ Reggae
☐ Rock & Roll
☐ Salsa
☐ Samba
☐ Saxophone
☐ Sitar
☐ Soul
☐ Soundtracks
☐ Steel Drums
☐ String Bands
☐ Swing
☐ Synthesizer
☐ Tango
☐ Trombone
☐ Trumpet
☐ Violin

**Who are her five favorite musicians /
musical artists?**

_____   _____   _____

_____   _____

Novelty & Obscure Gifts

These gifts run the gamut. You can buy anything from a ten-foot statue of a praying mantis to a twenty-pound wooden rooster. Why? I have no idea but these items are out there if you want them. Although impossible to list even a fraction of conceivable novelty items, hopefully the following list contains a few ideas to spark your imagination. Just pick a novelty theme and go hunting. Odds are, you can find exactly what you are looking for.

☐ Gumball Machine
☐ Stuffed Animals
☐ Giant Candy Cane
☐ American Flag Lights
☐ Funny Pens
☐ Safari Hat
☐ Personalized Mugs
☐ Giant Snowman
☐ Lawn Jockey
☐ Pine Cone Basket
☐ Snow Globe
☐ Animal Horns
☐ Animal Heads
☐ Feather Lamp Shade
☐ Goofy Shower Curtain
☐ Fluorescent Black Lights
☐ Crazy Hats
☐ Medieval Catapult
☐ Fart Machine
☐ Mirror Ball
☐ Fiber Optic Lamp
☐ Spinning Party Light
☐ Crystal Ball
☐ Locomotive Bank

☐ Stain Glass Butterflies
☐ Sleeping Cat Paperweight
☐ Pewter Frog Pendant
☐ Train Whistle
☐ Downspout Gargoyle
☐ Trophy Lamps
☐ Scrolling Message Hat
☐ Decorative Masks
☐ Wacky Soaps
☐ Ceramic Toads
☐ Lady Justice Statue
☐ Pair of Brass Hands
☐ Plastic Ballerina Statue
☐ Zen Gardens
☐ Lighted Ice Cubes
☐ Eye Chart
☐ Frog Lamp
☐ Dragons
☐ Red Feather Tree
☐ Puppets
☐ Wizard Fantasy Knife
☐ Floating Plastic Fish

☐ IQ Test
☐ Novelty Book
☐ Temporary Tattoos
☐ Tabletop Rock Garden
☐ Glowing Pebbles
☐ Refrigerator Magnet
☐ Yard Gnome
☐ Sculptures
☐ Statues
☐ Vases
☐ Carvings
☐ Toys
☐ Stuffed Animals
☐ Glass Figurines
☐ Life Size Chess Set
☐ Animal Wall Sconces
☐ Fuzzy Dice
☐ Peacock Feathers
☐ Fake Tatoos
☐ Masks
☐ Skeletons
☐ Suit of Armor
☐ Bobble Head Dolls
☐ Taxidermy Animals
☐ Tin Signs

Office Supplies

There are more professional and powerful women in the work force every day. It is highly probable those very same women would love well thought-out gifts from one of the many office supply stores. It doesn't hurt that these are probably your favorite stores too.

- ☐ Mail Holder
- ☐ Business Card Holder
- ☐ File Cabinet
- ☐ Office Telephone
- ☐ Headset
- ☐ Desk
- ☐ Shelving
- ☐ Computer Table
- ☐ Computer
- ☐ Desk Lamp
- ☐ Floor Lamp
- ☐ Roller Chair
- ☐ Printer
- ☐ Paper Shredder
- ☐ Envelopes
- ☐ High-backed Chair
- ☐ Ergonomic Chair
- ☐ Three Ring Binders
- ☐ Magazine Rack
- ☐ Stapler
- ☐ CD Holder
- ☐ Copy Paper
- ☐ Photographic Paper
- ☐ Computer Labels
- ☐ Tape Dispenser
- ☐ Stationary
- ☐ Bulletin Board
- ☐ Paper Clips

- ☐ Printer Cartridges
- ☐ Conference Table
- ☐ Chairs
- ☐ Mouse Pad
- ☐ Mouse
- ☐ Ruler
- ☐ Calculator
- ☐ Scissors
- ☐ Pens
- ☐ Pencils
- ☐ Fireproof Safe
- ☐ Drafting Table
- ☐ Trash Can
- ☐ Vertical Files
- ☐ Storage Racks
- ☐ Work Lamp
- ☐ Magnetic Notice Board
- ☐ Cabinets
- ☐ Bookcase
- ☐ Wall Clock
- ☐ Plants
- ☐ Batteries
- ☐ Binders
- ☐ Briefcase
- ☐ Business Cards
- ☐ Calendar
- ☐ Chalk & Erasers
- ☐ Chalk Board
- ☐ Clipboard
- ☐ Copier

- ☐ Scanner
- ☐ Correction Fluid
- ☐ Desk Organizer
- ☐ Desk Accessories
- ☐ Drafting Supplies
- ☐ Diskettes
- ☐ Dry-erase Board
- ☐ Dry-erase Markers
- ☐ Easels
- ☐ Surge Protector
- ☐ Fan
- ☐ Air Purifier
- ☐ Fasteners
- ☐ Fax Machine
- ☐ Fax Paper
- ☐ First Aid Supplies
- ☐ Forms
- ☐ Glue
- ☐ Highlighter
- ☐ Index Cards
- ☐ Rolodex
- ☐ Label Maker
- ☐ Labeling Tape
- ☐ Multi-purpose Labels
- ☐ Computer Labels
- ☐ Legal Kits
- ☐ Letter Opener
- ☐ Notebooks
- ☐ Mailing Supplies
- ☐ Message Pad

- Notepad
- Personal Organizer
- Paper Punch
- Recorder
- Ribbons
- Report Covers
- Rubber Bands
- Sheet Protectors
- Sorters
- Stamps
- Stamp Pads
- Staple Remover
- Stapler
- Wrist Rest
- Books on Success
- Mini Refrigerator
- Bookends
- Desk Clock
- Pencil Cup
- Memo Holder
- Paperweight
- Scratch Pads
- Drawing Pads
- Message Books
- Postal Scales
- Three Hole Punch
- Tape Dispenser
- Tape
- Packaging Tape
- Push Pins
- Dictionary
- Zip Code Directory
- Coin Sorter
- Road Atlas
- Cash Box
- Financial Books
- Laminator
- Thesaurus
- Paper Fasteners
- Color Paper
- Mini Stapler
- Coated Paper Clips
- Binder Clips
- Rubber Bands
- Keyboard Dust Cover
- Computer Dust Cover
- Letterhead Envelopes
- Letterhead Stationary
- Day Planners
- Personal Data Accessories
- Letter Opener
- Copy Machine
- Electric Pencil Sharpener
- Notebook
- Lunch Bags
- Glue
- Super Glue
- Cash Box
- Business Computer Software
- Rotary File
- Index Cards
- Bookends
- Chair Mat
- Wrist Guard
- Permanent Markers
- Crayons
- Water Soluble Markers
- Mini Tape Recorder
- Calculator
- Electronic Translator
- Telephone Extension Cord
- Video Conference Phone
- Projector
- Zip Drive
- Electric Bill Counter
- Multimedia Projector

Outdoors

Ah, there is nothing better than the great outdoors. If your honey enjoys gardening or just recreating under the big blue sky, find something from the following list to make her smile.

- ☐ Picnic Basket
- ☐ Thermometer
- ☐ Planter Boxes
- ☐ Vegetable Seeds
- ☐ Flower Seeds
- ☐ Bench
- ☐ Patio Furniture
- ☐ Binoculars
- ☐ Watering Hose
- ☐ Watering Pale
- ☐ Books on Gardening
- ☐ Walkway Lighting
- ☐ Solar Powered Lighting
- ☐ Greenhouse
- ☐ Coy Pond
- ☐ Build a Stone Walkway
- ☐ Gardening Tools
- ☐ Fountain
- ☐ Rock Garden
- ☐ Hammock
- ☐ Swing Set
- ☐ Porch Swing
- ☐ Plant Mister
- ☐ Aerating Shoes
- ☐ Garden Fence
- ☐ Soft Garden Cushion
- ☐ Beach Blanket
- ☐ Beach Towel

- ☐ Beach Toys
- ☐ Pool Furniture
- ☐ Pool Toys and Games
- ☐ Swimming Pool
- ☐ Tent
- ☐ Camping Gear
- ☐ Fencing
- ☐ Fire Pit
- ☐ Lawn Furniture
- ☐ Hammock
- ☐ Hot Tub
- ☐ Patio Heater
- ☐ Welcome Mat
- ☐ Metal Detector
- ☐ Traditional Bird Feeder
- ☐ Hummingbird Feeder
- ☐ Sunscreen
- ☐ Copper Lanterns
- ☐ Garden Hose Coiler
- ☐ Inflatable Swimming Pool
- ☐ Swimming Pool Rafts
- ☐ Pool Chairs
- ☐ Heat Lamp
- ☐ Novelty Mail Box
- ☐ Log Crib
- ☐ Collapsible Ladder

- ☐ Patio Furniture
- ☐ Patio Furniture Covers
- ☐ New Cushions
- ☐ Cedar Arbor
- ☐ Lattice Screen
- ☐ New Plantings
- ☐ Storage Bench
- ☐ Gazebo
- ☐ Patio Table Umbrella
- ☐ Picnic Table
- ☐ Fountains
- ☐ Wall Gardens
- ☐ Hanging Baskets
- ☐ Water Garden
- ☐ Large Imitation Rocks
- ☐ Outdoor Fireplace
- ☐ Outdoor Speakers
- ☐ Barbecue Grill
- ☐ Outdoor Games
- ☐ Bird Bath
- ☐ Plants
- ☐ Vines
- ☐ Trees
- ☐ Flowers
- ☐ Misc. Swimming Pool Supplies
- ☐ Misc. Gardening Supplies

Personalized Gifts

You can put her name, her initials, or her likeness on just about anything. You can embroider, emboss, print, sew, and engrave many items to customize them especially for her. And don't think these personalized gifts stop with her name or initials. You can personalize the following gifts with her nickname, a pet's name, a boat's name, a special date, a commemorative event, a favorite poem, quote, or any other identifying phrase to create fun and original gift ideas.

☐ Stationery
☐ Envelopes
☐ Thank You Notes
☐ Business Cards
☐ Mailing Labels
☐ Return Address Labels
☐ Stickers
☐ Pens
☐ Pencils
☐ Golf Tees
☐ Golf Towels
☐ Misc. Athletic Equipment
☐ Note Pads
☐ Sketch Pads
☐ Tee Shirts
☐ Towels
☐ Bathrobe
☐ Slippers
☐ Hats
☐ Director's Chair

☐ Stamps
☐ Buttons / Pins
☐ Pocket Knife
☐ Trophies
☐ Plaques
☐ Lighter
☐ Ash Tray
☐ Coin Purse
☐ Wallet
☐ Purse
☐ Briefcase
☐ Luggage
☐ Christmas Ornaments
☐ Flask
☐ Shot Glasses
☐ Drink Glasses
☐ Key Chain
☐ Wine Labels
☐ Dessert Plates
☐ Coffee Mugs
☐ Utensils

☐ Picture Frames
☐ Ceramic Pots
☐ Vases
☐ Refrigerator Magnets
☐ Calendars
☐ Bicycle Water Bottle
☐ Stuffed Animals
☐ Storage Box
☐ Photo Album
☐ Vanity License Plates
☐ Tool Box
☐ Jewelry Box
☐ Bed Liners
☐ Books
☐ Journals
☐ Jewelry

Pets

Pets are like babies to their owners. Just like buying gifts for mommies, gifts for a woman's pet can be truly appreciated. Since your goal is to deepen her love for you, don't forget to take care of Fluffy, the other love of her life. And remember, odds are she will dump you before she dumps the mutt.

- ☐ New Leash
- ☐ Scratcher
- ☐ New Collar
- ☐ New Houses
- ☐ New Cages
- ☐ New Aquariums
- ☐ Play Toy
- ☐ Chew Toy
- ☐ Tasty Treats
- ☐ Playpen
- ☐ Blanket
- ☐ Pet Pillow
- ☐ Pet Bed
- ☐ Hair Brush
- ☐ Radio Fence
- ☐ Shirt
- ☐ Sweater
- ☐ Bandana
- ☐ Behavioral School
- ☐ Flea / Tick Treatment
- ☐ Designer Food Dish
- ☐ Designer Water Bowl
- ☐ Anti-bark Collar
- ☐ Build a Pet Ramp
- ☐ Another Pet for Companionship
- ☐ Plaster Tile Kit for Paw Prints
- ☐ New Litter Box or Poop Scoop
- ☐ Pet Grooming Kit
- ☐ Pet Life Vest for Swimming
- ☐ Food Bin
- ☐ Professional Grooming Services
- ☐ Pet Sling
- ☐ Travel Inflatable Bowl
- ☐ A New Castle for her Gold Fish
- ☐ Pet Carrier
- ☐ Travel Pet Blanket
- ☐ Automatic Pet Feeder
- ☐ Collapsible Dog Bowl
- ☐ Scratching Post
- ☐ Kennel
- ☐ Ultrasonic Dog Barking Trainer
- ☐ Heating
- ☐ Vehicle Safety Harness
- ☐ Pet Medication
- ☐ ID Tags
- ☐ Vitamins
- ☐ Books on Pets
- ☐ Gates
- ☐ Novelty Items
- ☐ Pet Portrait
- ☐ Pet Car Seat
- ☐ Computer Chip Identification

WARNING!

Do not buy a gift for Fluffy and forget to buy a gift for the girl.
You will quickly find yourself in the dog house.

Safety & Survival

Each area of the country has its own emergency needs.
The plains states are concerned with tornados while
California worries about the big earthquake. Florida and
the Eastern seaboard constantly peer into the ocean for
hurricanes and snow blankets the Northern states every
year.   In the desert states like Arizona, the sun can be a
formidable enemy. Hazards even plague every day life
through normal accidents and criminal activity.   How

comforting will it be for her to own the tools to get her out of any emergency situation?

Many of the following are useful and needed in every day life. Others are used in extreme emergencies. Whether she ever uses the items or not, she will appreciate you thinking about her safety.

- ☐ Flashlights
- ☐ Earthquake Lights
- ☐ Extra Batteries
- ☐ Portable Generator
- ☐ Cellular Telephone
- ☐ Emergency Candles
- ☐ Cellular Telephone Headset
- ☐ Automotive Cellular Charger
- ☐ Lighter
- ☐ Waterproof Matches
- ☐ Windproof Matches
- ☐ Windshield Hammer
- ☐ First Aid Kit
- ☐ Key Chain Flash Light
- ☐ Portable Radio
- ☐ Duct Tape
- ☐ Compass
- ☐ Night Vision Goggles
- ☐ Escape Chain Ladder

- ☐ Fire / Smoke Breathing Hood
- ☐ Gas Mask
- ☐ Pepper Spray
- ☐ Pepper Foam
- ☐ Plastic Sheeting
- ☐ Earthquake Preparedness Kit
- ☐ Tire Foam
- ☐ Magnesium Fire Starter
- ☐ Gun Lock
- ☐ Survival Books
- ☐ Self Defense Classes
- ☐ Shovel for Car
- ☐ Rope for Car
- ☐ Life Jacket
- ☐ Magnifying Glass
- ☐ Two-Way Radios
- ☐ Emergency Survival Blanket
- ☐ Whistle
- ☐ Plastic Sheeting
- ☐ Water Purification Kit
- ☐ Emergency Strobe Light
- ☐ Chemical Glow Sticks
- ☐ Rope
- ☐ Wrist Guards

- ☐ Global Positioning System
- ☐ Thermometer
- ☐ Blood Pressure Monitor
- ☐ Cholesterol Monitor
- ☐ Blood Alcohol Detector
- ☐ Latex Gloves
- ☐ Work Gloves
- ☐ Gun Lock
- ☐ Flares
- ☐ Vehicle Anti-theft Device
- ☐ Sun Block
- ☐ Protective Eyewear
- ☐ Fire Extinguisher
- ☐ Carbon Monoxide Detector
- ☐ Multi-function Pocket Knife
- ☐ Emergency Tool Kit
- ☐ Auto Club Enrollment
- ☐ Reflector Pants
- ☐ Survival Foods
- ☐ Traffic Wand

> **If there was a choice between safety and romance, I am not sure women would pick safety.**

Sexual & Sensual

If ever there was a gift to give your lover that was like giving a gift to yourself, this is it. Sex and sensuality are an important part of any relationship. The more you reward your partner with sensual gifts the more likely you will be rewarded in return. An added bonus for you men is the romantic nature of these gifts. Use them creatively in conjunction with other gifts to make her feel loved and appreciated. In turn, she might appreciate you all the more.

- ☐ Dual Shower Heads
- ☐ Water Massager
- ☐ Soft Body Buffers
- ☐ Big Comfy Bath Towels
- ☐ Lingerie
- ☐ Silk Sheets
- ☐ Incense & Burner
- ☐ Scented Candles
- ☐ Floating Candles
- ☐ Massage Oils
- ☐ Massage Table
- ☐ Bubble Bath Soaps
- ☐ Personal Lubricants
- ☐ Adult Toys
- ☐ Adult Videos
- ☐ Jacuzzi
- ☐ Aromatherapy Scents
- ☐ "Better Sex" Books
- ☐ "Better Sex" Videos
- ☐ Favorite Wine or Spirit
- ☐ Romantic CD
- ☐ Sensual Foods
- ☐ Down Comforter
- ☐ Big Fluffy Pillows
- ☐ Flower Pedals
- ☐ Bathing Glove
- ☐ Comfy Lounging Clothes
- ☐ Foot Massagers
- ☐ Neck Massagers
- ☐ Floor Pillows
- ☐ Big Comfy Robes
- ☐ Book of Poetry
- ☐ Lounging Furniture
- ☐ Books on Romance

Software

Computers have become part of mainstream society. Almost every household and business has them. Fifty years ago computers did not even exist. Imagine the things computers will do for us as the years progress. The following list breaks down computer software into categories. Look through them and see if the woman in your life has any use for a few new programs.

- Business
- Graphics
- Education
- Handheld Computing
- Personal Interest
- Tax Preparation
- Finance
- Operating Systems
- Accounting
- Web Development
- Contact Management
- Screenwriting
- Foreign Language Teaching
- Photography
- Database Management
- Print Creativity
- Artwork
- Anti Virus Programs
- Musical Instrument Instruction
- Computer Games
- Computer Virus Protection
- Firewall
- Pop-up Add Blocking
- Desktop Publishing
- Reference
- Presentation Assistance
- Project Management
- Spreadsheets
- Word Processing
- Voice Recognition
- Mapping Software
- Photo Editing
- Video Editing
- Computer Aided Design
- Backup Software
- Security
- Clip Art
- New Fonts
- Screen Savers

Sports & Athletic Equipment

Well fellas, here is a category we have a lot of knowledge and interest in. But we are not the only ones. More and more women take part in athletics and have as much interest in sports as the most diehard man. For those women, the following list is chock full of ideas. And the great thing about buying sporting equipment for them is the experience of going to our favorite stores as well. Yahoo!

Baseball
- Baseball Bat
- Batting Glove
- Baseball
- Softball
- Bags
- Pitching Machine
- Rebounder
- Practice Net

Basketball

- ☐ Basketball
- ☐ Backboard
- ☐ Portable Backboard
- ☐ Basket Rim Net

Billiards

- ☐ Pool Table
- ☐ Cue Sticks
- ☐ Balls
- ☐ Cue Stick Case

Boating

- ☐ Speed Boat
- ☐ Canoe
- ☐ Rowboat
- ☐ Kayak
- ☐ Rafts
- ☐ Motor
- ☐ Boat Carrier
- ☐ Helmets
- ☐ Life Vests
- ☐ Paddles
- ☐ Trolling Motor
- ☐ Marine Hardware
- ☐ Electronics
- ☐ Boat Covers
- ☐ Coolers
- ☐ Marine Accessories
- ☐ Dry Bags

Body Boarding

- ☐ Board
- ☐ Wet Suit
- ☐ Gloves
- ☐ Booties
- ☐ Surf Fins

Bowling

- ☐ Bowling Ball
- ☐ Tote Bags
- ☐ Glove
- ☐ Bowling Shoes
- ☐ Towel
- ☐ Ball Polisher
- ☐ Rosin Bag

Climbing

- ☐ Ropes
- ☐ Helmet
- ☐ Bags
- ☐ Brake Bar
- ☐ Climbing Shoes
- ☐ GPS Unit
- ☐ Altimeter
- ☐ Two Way Radio
- ☐ Climbing Harness
- ☐ Ice Axe
- ☐ Trekking Pole
- ☐ Chalk Bag
- ☐ Folding Shovel
- ☐ Carabiners
- ☐ Pulleys
- ☐ Stopper Nuts

Cycling

- ☐ Mountain Bike
- ☐ Racing Bike
- ☐ BMX Bike
- ☐ Multi-speed Bicycle
- ☐ Unicycle
- ☐ Helmets
- ☐ Cycling Shoes
- ☐ Cycling Gloves
- ☐ Water Bottles
- ☐ Lights
- ☐ Mirrors
- ☐ Reflection Devices

- ☐ Bicycle Lock
- ☐ Protective Gear
- ☐ Tires
- ☐ Bicycle Repairing Kit
- ☐ Automotive Bike Rack
- ☐ Storage Bike Rack
- ☐ New Seat
- ☐ Seat Cushion

Exercise

- ☐ Weights
- ☐ Racks
- ☐ Weight Bench
- ☐ Treadmill
- ☐ Stopwatch
- ☐ Trampoline
- ☐ Stepper
- ☐ Exercise Bike
- ☐ Climbing Machine
- ☐ Step Machine
- ☐ Rowing Machine
- ☐ Home Gym
- ☐ Fitness Ball
- ☐ Exercise Mat
- ☐ Yoga Mat
- ☐ Aquatic Barbells
- ☐ Scales
- ☐ Monitors
- ☐ Nutritional Supplements
- ☐ Jump Ropes
- ☐ Inversion Equipment
- ☐ Pedometer
- ☐ Ankle Weights
- ☐ Weight Belt

Fishing
- [ ] Fly Fishing Rod
- [ ] Fly Fishing Reel
- [ ] Spinning Rod
- [ ] Spinning Reel
- [ ] Lures
- [ ] Fishing Line
- [ ] Fish Finder
- [ ] Polarized Sunglasses
- [ ] Nets
- [ ] Fishing Tackle
- [ ] Tackle Box
- [ ] Waders
- [ ] Fishing Vests
- [ ] Digital Scale
- [ ] Fishing Boat
- [ ] Trolling Motor
- [ ] Depth Finder
- [ ] Dry Bags
- [ ] Filet Knife
- [ ] Scaling Knife

Football
- [ ] Football
- [ ] Helmet
- [ ] Face Mask
- [ ] Mouth Guard
- [ ] Shoulder Pads
- [ ] Protective Gear
- [ ] Scrimmage Vests
- [ ] Football Jersey

Golf
- [ ] Golf Clubs
- [ ] Golf Bag
- [ ] Shoes
- [ ] Golf Cart
- [ ] Pull Cart
- [ ] Gloves
- [ ] Putter
- [ ] Tees
- [ ] Rangefinder
- [ ] Head Covers
- [ ] Practice Putting Mat
- [ ] New Grips
- [ ] Golf Balls
- [ ] Golf Attire

Hiking & Camping
- [ ] Hiking Staff
- [ ] Backpacks
- [ ] Waist Packs
- [ ] Tent
- [ ] Sleeping Bag
- [ ] Blankets
- [ ] Cooler
- [ ] Air Mattress
- [ ] Lanterns
- [ ] First Aid Kit
- [ ] Water Treatment Kit
- [ ] Binoculars
- [ ] GPS Equipment
- [ ] Maps
- [ ] Nature Guide
- [ ] Outdoor Cookware
- [ ] Outdoor Cooking Stove
- [ ] Fuel
- [ ] Headlamp
- [ ] Survival Gear

Hockey
- [ ] Hockey Ice Skates
- [ ] Roller Skates
- [ ] Pucks
- [ ] Sticks
- [ ] Gloves
- [ ] Goals
- [ ] Helmet
- [ ] Mouth Guards
- [ ] Gear Bags
- [ ] Gloves
- [ ] Masks
- [ ] Shields
- [ ] Shin Guards
- [ ] Other Protective Gear

Hunting
- [ ] Rifle
- [ ] Bow
- [ ] Arrows
- [ ] Cross Bow
- [ ] Ammunition
- [ ] Binoculars
- [ ] Decoys
- [ ] Hunting Dog
- [ ] Game Calls
- [ ] Night Vision
- [ ] Equipment
- [ ] Gun Cases
- [ ] Gun Locks
- [ ] Rangefinders
- [ ] Scents
- [ ] Lures
- [ ] Scopes
- [ ] Calls
- [ ] Practice Targets
- [ ] Tree Stands
- [ ] Warmers
- [ ] Knives
- [ ] Holsters
- [ ] Animal Traps
- [ ] Eye Protection
- [ ] Hearing Protection
- [ ] Gun Cleaning Kit
- [ ] Binoculars

Martial Arts
- ☐ Gloves
- ☐ Head Gear
- ☐ Protective Gear
- ☐ Belts
- ☐ Heavy Bag
- ☐ Speed Bag
- ☐ Kidney Protector
- ☐ Body Shield
- ☐ Chest Protector
- ☐ Shin Guard
- ☐ Mouth Guard
- ☐ Exercise Mat
- ☐ Medicine Ball
- ☐ Weaponry

Paintball
- ☐ Paintball Gun
- ☐ Paintballs
- ☐ Duffel Bags
- ☐ Hoppers
- ☐ Loaders
- ☐ Protection Gear
- ☐ Compressed Air Tanks
- ☐ Two-way Radios
- ☐ Camouflage Gear

Running
- ☐ Footwear
- ☐ Apparel
- ☐ Reflective Gear
- ☐ Sports Watch
- ☐ Pedometer
- ☐ Jogging Stroller
- ☐ Water Bottle
- ☐ Waist Pack

Scuba Diving
- ☐ Mask
- ☐ Snorkel
- ☐ Fins
- ☐ Booties
- ☐ Gloves
- ☐ Neoprene Wet Suit
- ☐ Lycra Body Suit
- ☐ First Stage
- ☐ Regulators
- ☐ Octopus Rig
- ☐ Gauges
- ☐ Buoyancy Control Device
- ☐ Dive Computer
- ☐ Underwater Navigation Compass
- ☐ Dive Knife
- ☐ Spare Air
- ☐ Compressed Air Tank
- ☐ Dive Bag
- ☐ Spear Gun
- ☐ Stringer
- ☐ Underwater Camera
- ☐ Underwater Flashlight
- ☐ Chemical Glow Sticks
- ☐ Diver's Insurance
- ☐ Diver Down Flag
- ☐ Underwater Propulsion
- ☐ Dive Watch

Skateboarding
- ☐ Skateboard
- ☐ Wheels
- ☐ Protective Gear
- ☐ Helmet
- ☐ Grind Rails
- ☐ Ramps

Skating
- ☐ Ice Skates
- ☐ Roller Skates
- ☐ In-line Skates
- ☐ Hockey Skates
- ☐ Figure Skates
- ☐ Helmets
- ☐ Knee Pads
- ☐ Wrist Guards
- ☐ Elbow Pads
- ☐ Skate Bags

Snorkeling
- ☐ Mask
- ☐ Snorkel
- ☐ Fins
- ☐ Booties
- ☐ Gloves

Snowboarding
- ☐ Snowboard
- ☐ Bindings
- ☐ Snowboard Boots
- ☐ Helmets
- ☐ Equipment Packs
- ☐ Goggles
- ☐ Protective Gear

Snow Skiing
- ☐ Downhill Skis
- ☐ Cross Country Skis
- ☐ Bindings
- ☐ Poles
- ☐ Boots
- ☐ Backpacks
- ☐ Waist Packs

☐ Goggles
☐ Helmets
☐ Equipment Bag
☐ Sunglasses
☐ Two-way Radio
☐ Ski Rack
☐ Ski Apparel
☐ Protective Gear
☐ Ski Wax
☐ GPS Equipment
☐ Avalanche
   Transceivers
☐ Altimeter

Soccer
☐ Soccer Ball
☐ Practice Goal
☐ Shin Guards
☐ Equipment Bags

Swimming
☐ Swim Suit
☐ Swim Cap
☐ Mask
☐ Goggles
☐ Fins
☐ Life Vests
☐ Sun Protection
   Products
☐ Buoyancy Belts

Surfing
☐ Surfboard
☐ Wet Suit
☐ Gloves

☐ Booties
☐ Wax

**Tennis &
Racquetball**
☐ Tennis Racquet
☐ Tennis Balls
☐ Headbands
☐ Wristbands
☐ Safety Glasses
☐ Visor
☐ Ball Machine
☐ Court Equipment
☐ Ball Hoppers
☐ Racquetball
   Racquet
☐ Racquetballs
☐ Eyewear
☐ Gloves
☐ Grips

Volleyball
☐ Volleyball Net
☐ Volleyball

Water Skiing
☐ Water Skis
☐ Slalom Ski
☐ Rope
☐ Handle
☐ Vests
☐ Wet Suit
☐ Booties
☐ Knee Board
☐ Wakeboard

☐ Inflatable Towing
   Tubes

**Misc. Athletic
Stuff**
☐ Books on Sports
☐ Athletic Apparel
   for Every Sport
☐ Backpacks
☐ Duffels
☐ Hats
☐ Ball Inflation
   Devices
☐ Athletic Footwear
☐ Sport Logo
   Apparel
☐ Sunglasses
☐ Sport Videos
☐ Sport Video
   Games
☐ Sport
   Memorabilia
☐ Sport Lessons
☐ Favorite Athlete
   Memorabilia
☐ Wrist Brace
☐ Back Brace
☐ Knee Brace
☐ Ankle Brace
☐ Athletic Tape
☐ Ice Packs
☐ Bandages
☐ Heat / Ice Kits

Things For The Single Mom

I believe single mothering to be one of the most difficult jobs around. Much of the time, a third of their income goes to daycare just so they can work in the first place. Take out another percentage for taxes and a huge chunk for their mortgage. What they are left with is very little to cover their kid's food, education, clothing, entertainment, and the like. Let alone, getting all those things for themselves.

And what about time? Single mothers must work all day while their children are in school, come home in time to prepare nutritious meals, spend quality time with the kids, and then struggle to get them to bed. After that, they are blessed with a few precious moments to clean the house and do whatever chores need to be done before collapsing in bed. It sounds unfathomable and it is. Imagine what a well thought-out gift would mean to these deserving women?

Things for Her

- ☐ Clothing
- ☐ Favorite Store Gift Certificates
- ☐ Shopping Spree
- ☐ Massage
- ☐ Spa Day
- ☐ Vacation
- ☐ Babysitting Services
- ☐ Maid Services
- ☐ Laundry Services
- ☐ Diaper Services
- ☐ Night on the Town
- ☐ Free Day To Run Errands
- ☐ Flowers Delivered To Her Work
- ☐ Anything She Would Not Buy For Herself
- ☐ Any Romantic Gifts
- ☐ Gardener
- ☐ Handyman for a day

Things for the Kids

- ☐ Baby Needs
- ☐ Children's Books
- ☐ Subscriptions
- ☐ Musical Lessons
- ☐ Fun Toys
- ☐ Educational Toys
- ☐ Casual Clothing
- ☐ School Supplies
- ☐ School Clothing
- ☐ Shoes
- ☐ Bunk Beds
- ☐ Child's Desk

- ☐ Night Lights
- ☐ New Bedding
- ☐ Movies

- ☐ Outdoor Playground Equipment

- ☐ Educational Software

Tools & Hardware

I realize it goes against every fiber of our being, but we must avoid this category in favor of the more romantic gifts. I realize it is packed with items we find genuinely wonderful and exciting, but romance to women is not a seventeen-inch, one and a half horsepower, sixteen-speed drill press with linear scale and a belt and pulley drive system. Go figure.

So facing that fact, any hardware item you can possibly think of should be used for her instead of given to her. Although a new lawn mower might be a great idea for you, it will in all probability mean very little to her. However, if you take that new mower over to her house and mow her lawn, now you might be on to something. The same goes for snow blowers, leaf blowers, chainsaws, and the like. As a general rule, this category is for action not for giving.

Travel

If travel plans have been made for both of you or even for her alone, it is important to think of items to help with her travel experience. Whether traveling to tourist destinations by plane or taking a trip off road into the wilderness, the following list contains items you can include in your gift-giving considerations.

- ☐ Maps
- ☐ Books on Destination

- ☐ Luggage Identifiers
- ☐ Luggage Strap

- ☐ Luggage
- ☐ Clothes Line
- ☐ Sun Glasses

- ☐ Camera Bag
- ☐ Camera Strap
- ☐ Extra Camera Battery
- ☐ Two-way Radios
- ☐ Travel Iron
- ☐ Travel Curling Iron
- ☐ Euro Currency Converter
- ☐ Battery Conversion Kit
- ☐ International Adapter
- ☐ Money Belt
- ☐ Travel Pillow
- ☐ Travel Alarm Clock
- ☐ Waist Pack
- ☐ Laundry Bag
- ☐ Waterproof Case
- ☐ Portable Fan
- ☐ Plastic Cooler
- ☐ Collapsible Soft Cooler
- ☐ Miniature Toiletries
- ☐ Blanket
- ☐ Beach Towel
- ☐ Toiletry Kit
- ☐ Sleeping Bag
- ☐ Sleeping Bag Liner
- ☐ Portable Toilet
- ☐ Travel Neck Wallet
- ☐ Multi-purpose Knife
- ☐ Blow Up Mattress
- ☐ Binoculars
- ☐ Designer Walking Stick
- ☐ 35mm Camera
- ☐ Digital Camera
- ☐ Travel Lock Box
- ☐ Luggage Lock
- ☐ Backpack
- ☐ Pedometer
- ☐ Waterproof Food Storage
- ☐ Mosquito Net
- ☐ First Aid Kit
- ☐ Folding Travel Chair
- ☐ Moist Towelettes
- ☐ Toilet Seat Covers
- ☐ Travel Mirror
- ☐ Trash Bags
- ☐ Outdoor Hanging Shower
- ☐ Inflatable Sink
- ☐ Sunglasses
- ☐ Sun Screen
- ☐ Sting lotion
- ☐ Snake Bite Kit
- ☐ Insect Repellent
- ☐ Hammock
- ☐ Water Purification Kit
- ☐ Flashlight
- ☐ Lantern
- ☐ Emergency Candles
- ☐ Flares
- ☐ Chemical Glowsticks
- ☐ Outdoor Blanket
- ☐ Waterproof Pen
- ☐ Waterproof Paper
- ☐ Travel Mug
- ☐ Bota Bag
- ☐ Emergency Strobe Light
- ☐ Cell Phone
- ☐ Travel Hair Drier
- ☐ Emergency Survival Blanket
- ☐ Chemical Hand Warmers
- ☐ Emergency Shovel
- ☐ Rain Gear
- ☐ Snow Gear
- ☐ Signal Whistle
- ☐ Magnesium Fire Starter
- ☐ Weather Gauge
- ☐ Global Positioning System
- ☐ Compass
- ☐ Travel Games
- ☐ Travel Reading Light
- ☐ Books on Tape
- ☐ Travel Cosmetic Case
- ☐ Lighted Travel Mirror
- ☐ Water Filled Travel Weights
- ☐ Collapsible Dog Bowl
- ☐ All Weather Travel Kit
- ☐ Waterproof Matches
- ☐ Severe Weather Travel Kit
- ☐ Spare Batteries

☐ Language
  Translation Book

☐ Document
  Storage Case

Various Leftovers

The following list contains a hodgepodge of items ranging in uses. Scan through the following to see if you find any additional surprises. Good hunting.

☐ Music Box
☐ Picture Holders
☐ Velvet Wine Bag
☐ Hangers
☐ Photo Albums
☐ Display Books
☐ Display Cabinets
☐ Seasonal Clothing
  Storage Bags
☐ Cedar Blocks
☐ Dish Racks
☐ Wine Tags
☐ Key Chain
☐ Pot Pourri Holder
☐ Personalized Mug
☐ Flask
☐ Lighter
☐ Photo Album
☐ Candle Holders
☐ Jewelry Boxes
☐ Personalized
  Trophy
☐ Humidor
☐ Cigar Cutter
☐ Wind Chimes
☐ New Doorbell
☐ Door Knocker
☐ Shower Rings
☐ Storage Canisters
☐ Lap Desk
☐ Train Set

☐ Dream Catcher
☐ Globe Liquor
  Caddy
☐ Globe of the
  World
☐ Hand Towels
☐ Bath Mats
☐ Assorted Vases
☐ Wigs
☐ Walking Stick
☐ Picnic Backpack
☐ Ultrasonic Pest
  Remover
☐ Water Filters
☐ Car Wash Kit
☐ Yoga Mat
☐ Balance Ball
☐ Magnifying Glass
☐ Calendars of
  Every Type
☐ Mini Refrigerator
☐ Mirrored
  Sunglasses
☐ Cooler
☐ Money Clip
☐ Clothing Steamer
☐ Vacuum Cleaner
☐ Hourglass
☐ Incense Burner
☐ Incense
☐ Compass

☐ Silver Goblets
☐ Merry Go Round
☐ Magic Trick Kit
☐ Lantern
☐ Weather Vane
☐ Duffel Bag
☐ Snoring Spray
☐ Massage Table
☐ Anti-Snoring
  Strips
☐ Airflow Pillow
☐ Inversion Table
☐ Teeth Whitening
  System
☐ Foot Supports
☐ Sun Tan Light
☐ Equipment Bags
☐ Sleeping Mat
☐ Cot
☐ Sleeping Bag
☐ Silk Flowers
☐ Silk Plants
☐ Stamp Box
☐ Armillary Sphere
☐ Kaleidoscope
☐ Bonsai Tree
☐ Pinball Machine
☐ Tripod
☐ Telescope
☐ Lens Cleaning Kit
☐ Camera Case

- [ ] Photo Albums
- [ ] Thimbles
- [ ] Brass Sextant
- [ ] World Atlas
- [ ] Spiritual Paraphernalia
- [ ] Seasonal Decorations
- [ ] Seasonal Candies
- [ ] Seasonal Foods
- [ ] Shoe Caddy
- [ ] Parachute
- [ ] Snow Sled
- [ ] Snowshoes
- [ ] Toboggan
- [ ] Prism
- [ ] Fantasy Chess Set
- [ ] Pressure Washing Hose
- [ ] Lobster Pot
- [ ] Crab Trap

WARNING!

Now that you have finished looking through the list, go back and review the items you checked off. Remember, this list is for her, not you. Omit all items you circled for yourself.

Chapter 29

Specific Gift List For The Uncreative Man

Take some time looking through the following list. Certainly this should provide some ready-made ideas to help let her know how much you care. You should consider altering the experience to match her unique likes and dislikes.

Event   Includes:

Theatre Experience: Dinner, theatre tickets, flowers, and maybe even a new dress for her to wear

Bed & Breakfast Getaway: Reservations at out-of-the-way Bed & Breakfast, luggage and car pre-packed, bottle of wine for the room, and her favorite snacks purchased for the road

Spa Day for Two: Reservations at a day spa for her and her best friend

Surprise Dinner for Two: Reservations at her favorite restaurant, babysitter pre-arranged, flowers, and a card

Day Trip to Local Winery: Reservations, complete set of crystal wine glasses, and gourmet cheese and crackers to accompany the purchased wine

Picnic Surprise: Make prior arrangements with her boss for extended lunch break, picnic basket filled with favorite foods and drink, romantic getaway spot, and flowers

Dinner and Jewelry: Romantic dinner for two at favorite Bistro and a surprise gift of jewelry between main and dessert courses

Home Movie Night: Arrange for kids to be out of the house, her favorite movie on DVD player, a nice bottle of wine, a comfy blanket, and her favorite snack

Portrait: Take her favorite picture of the both of you to a local artist. Have him paint, or sketch (less expensive), a portrait and surprise her with it on an important anniversary

Romantic Dinner Cruise: Reservations on the ship, flowers, and motion sickness pills should they be necessary prior to departing

Out-of-town Getaway: Hotel reservations, spa reservations, and dinner at an upscale restaurant. Have a few activities planned for the following day. Either let her pick her favorite activities or surprise her with ideas of your own.

Bath Experience: Fifty lit candles, pre-run bubble bath, incense, her favorite soft music, and pre-cut tropical fruits on a plate

Surprise Reunion: Arrangements for friends from out of town to come in on special day, dinner event to surprise her with reunion, and prearranged spa plans for the group the following day

Award Celebration: Novelty trophy for some accomplishment, reservations for dinner with family and friends, presentation of award and speech.

Pro Sporting Event: Tickets, team paraphernalia, and tailgating supplies

Amphitheatre Excursion: Picnic Basket filled with goodies, a warm blanket, and tickets if necessary

Gift Basket of Romance: Basket filled with flowers, gourmet candy, perfume, and a card telling her what she means to you

Gift Basket for the Bath: Basket filled with her favorite soaps, gels, bubble bath, bath beads, scented candles, her favorite CD, and a card

Gift Basket of Love: Basket filled with everything needed for an "adult" evening of entertainment. Oils, lotions, toys, and the like

Gift Basket of Taste: Basket filled with her favorite candies, cookies, liquor, and a note about dinner reservations at her favorite restaurant

Gift Basket of Touch: Basket filled with big fluffy bath towel, silk bathrobe, her favorite skin lotions, and an appointment card for professional massage

Gift Basket of Sound: Basket filled with new CD from several of her favorite artists, a portable CD player, headphones, and a mini tape recorder complete with pre-recorded message of love from you

Gift Basket of Smell: Basket filled with scented candles, incense, body sprays, scented lotions, and flowers

Flower Day: A different flower or bouquet of flowers in every room of the house along with a different heart-felt card next to each bouquet

Three Day Cruise: Ship reservations, a bottle of champagne for the cabin, motion sickness pills, and pre-purchased sandals, swimwear, and deck clothing for her on board

Burning Basket: Basket filled with clothing and/or novelty items you own which embarrass her, and a card telling her she may burn each item. You may include stick matches, lighter fluid, and marshmallows for roasting over the bonfire.

Post Pregnancy Basket: Basket filled with useful and humorous items for use after the pregnancy like miniature bottles of her favorite liquors, stress formula vitamins, sleep aids, books on child rearing, earplugs, and condoms to prevent other pregnancies

Sushi Basket: Basket filled with everything she needs to make sushi at home. Seaweed wraps, dry wasabi mustard, bag of rice, bamboo sushi roller, bottle of soy sauce, chopsticks, and fortune cookies.

Gift of Entertainment: Gift box filled with any combination of her five favorite movies of all time, a juicy novel, a magazine subscription, a book of crossword puzzles, CD's from one of her five favorite artists, and a bag of popcorn or some other snacks

Rock and Roll Night: Tickets to concert of her favorite band, container filled with favorite liquor, tee-shirts and other groupie paraphernalia, and the bands newest CD

Shopping Spree: Gift certificates from several of her favorite clothing stores, shoe stores, and home furnishing stores.

Chapter 30

Important Dates

Use the following list to jot down any important days you need to remember. Refer to this from time to time to make sure you do not have any upcoming events that have slipped your mind.

Valentine's Day   February 14th.

Mother's Day   _____

Christmas Day   December 25th.

Her Birthday   _____

Your Anniversary   _____

Her Family's Birthdays
   Mother   _____

   Father   _____

_____   _____

_____   _____

Her Pet's Birthday   _____

Other dates you need to remember:

_____   _____

_____   _____

_____   _____

_____   _____

_____   _____

_____   _____

Chapter 31

Thoughts, Hints, Wish Lists and Notes

If you have learned anything from this book, you know you must listen carefully to your partner. Throughout the year she will drop hints, make requests, and wish out loud for things she desires. Make immediate mental notes of these items until you have the opportunity to write them down. Also, as you develop your gift giving skills, you will create ideas of your own. Many unique ideas will likely pop into your head from out of the blue. Don't thrust them aside thinking you will remember them when gift time rolls around. Use the spaces below to jot down ideas you come up with or ideas she slides by you. All you need to do then is refer back to your notes prior to any gift-giving event. You may already have all the gift giving ideas you need.

Notes:

Notes:

_____

_____

_____

_____

_____

_____

_____

_____

_____

_____

_____

_____

_____

_____

_____

_____

_____

_____

_____

_____

_____

_____

_____

CONCLUSION

To put it very simply, anyone can be a good gift giver. It takes two things: A desire to show your significant other how much you care and a little knowledge of who she really is. Once you have those two elements, gift giving should become second nature to you.

You are not expected to give a gift for every possible occasion. You would be doing little else with your time. But remember, the more you give, the more she will feel loved.

To all those women who think their man is hopeless, give him time. Changing behavior does not happen overnight. Especially since shopping goes against his very nature. Do not keep him in the dark as to your likes and dislikes. Help him know what turns you on and more importantly what turns you off. Give him positive feedback when he succeeds in giving superior gifts. It is up to you to help nurture this young but developing skill. If you do not water and feed his growing desire, it will surely curl up and die.

For you men out there, take the time to fill in the questions. Do not be shy about asking her to help. She will no doubt enjoy the receiving end. And remember, this book is here for you when you have difficulty remembering those items most important to her. Keep it handy for those obligatory days as they come back around all too quickly. Keep it up to date as your sweetheart's likes and dislikes change. Use it as you need to for quick last minute gifts as well as for those important plan-intensive ones.

By now, you have undoubtedly figured out the added bonus to this book. It will not only help you buy gifts for your significant other, but it will make coming up with ideas for friends and family much easier too.

The goal of this book is to make gift giving far less painful for you and much more rewarding for her. As your skill level increases, gift-giving ideas not within these pages should strike a chord and you will likely come to the realization, "Wow, she would love this." You know you are getting better when this starts happening. Ultimately, if this book makes even one holiday more enjoyable for you and your significant other, it is a rousing success.

<u>Note To Readers</u>

Should you have any additions to the gift lists or stories you would like to share, please feel free to send them to me at Shanem Publishing. No promises, but I will try to use as many of them as possible in the new editions of this book.

Index

Gift Giving Handbook Order Form

Order online at: www.giftgivinghandbook.com

Postal Orders send check to: Shanem Publishing
                                          8491 Sunset Blvd., Box 1700-A
                                          West Hollywood, CA   90069
                                          USA

FAX Orders to: (818) 763-9166

Name: _____

Company: _____

Address: _____

City: _____ State: _____ Zip code: _____-_____

Telephone: (___) _____

Number of books: _____

Cost per book: $12.95

Sales Tax: Please add 8.25% ($1.07 per book) for books only
                          shipped to addresses in California

Shipping: Surface Rate is $2.50 for the first book and $1.00
                          for each additional book. Allow two to four weeks
                          for surface shipping. Air Rate is $3.75 per book

Total Cost: _____ X $12.95 = _____ + _____ + _____ = _____
                 Number of books   Sales Tax   Shipping   Total

Payment Method   _____Visa _____MasterCard _____American Express

Card Number: _____ Expiration Date: _____

Name on Card: _____